Reform Doesn't Work

OTHER ROWMAN & LITTLEFIELD EDUCATION BOOKS BY KEEN BABBAGE

High Impact Teaching: Overcoming Student Apathy
Extreme Teaching
Extreme Students: Challenging All Students and Energizing Learning
Results-Driven Teaching: Teach So Well That Every Student Learns
Extreme Economics: The Need for Personal Finance in the School Curriculum
What Only Teachers Know About Education: The Reality of the Classroom
Extreme Economics: Teaching Children and Teenagers About Money, Second Edition
Extreme Writing: Discovering the Writer in Every Student
The Extreme Principle: What Matters Most, What Works Best
The Dream and the Reality of Teaching: Becoming the Best Teacher Students Ever Had

Reform Doesn't Work

Grassroots Efforts Can Provide Answers to School Improvement

Keen Babbage

ROWMAN & LITTLEFIELD EDUCATION
A division of
ROWMAN & LITTLEFIELD PUBLISHERS, INC.
Lanham • New York • Toronto • Plymouth, UK

Published by Rowman & Littlefield Education
A division of Rowman & Littlefield Publishers, Inc.
A wholly owned subsidiary of The Rowman & Littlefield Publishing Group, Inc.
4501 Forbes Boulevard, Suite 200, Lanham, Maryland 20706
www.rowman.com

10 Thornbury Road
Plymouth PL6 7PP
United Kingdom

Copyright © 2012 by Keen Babbage

All rights reserved. No part of this book may be reproduced in any form or by any electronic or mechanical means, including information storage and retrieval systems, without written permission from the publisher, except by a reviewer who may quote passages in a review.

British Library Cataloguing in Publication Information Available

Library of Congress Cataloging-in-Publication Data

Babbage, Keen J.
  Reform doesn't work : grassroots efforts can provide answers to school improvement / Keen Babbage.
    p. cm.
  ISBN 978-1-61048-615-6 (cloth : alk. paper)—ISBN 978-1-61048-616-3 (pbk. : alk. paper)—ISBN 978-1-61048-617-0 (electronic)
  1. School improvement programs—United States. 2. Community and school—United States. 3. Public schools—United States—Citizen participation. 4. Educational change—United States. I. Title.
  LB2822.82.B325 2012
  371.2'07—dc23
                                                            2012000351

∞™ The paper used in this publication meets the minimum requirements of American National Standard for Information Sciences—Permanence of Paper for Printed Library Materials, ANSI/NISO Z39.48-1992.

Printed in the United States of America

Dedicated to my family

Contents

Preface	ix
Acknowledgments	xi
1 Everyone	1
2 Parents and Guardians	19
3 Community Groups	35
4 Media	47
5 Elected Officials, Candidates for Public Office, Politicians	61
6 Voters, Citizens, Taxpayers	75
7 The National Government and State Governments	87
8 Businesses and Business Advocacy Groups	99
9 Students	113
10 Former Educators	125
11 Current Educators	137
12 The Power of Shared School Purpose	147
13 The Great Debate: The Reformers Respond and the Grass Roots Reply	157
About the Author	169

Preface

This book was written in June and July of 2011, soon after the 2010–11 school year ended. It was an unusual school year because I had to miss half of it.

On October 12 of that school year, I was diagnosed with sinus cancer. I had to tell the students on October 13 that I would be gone for a long time. My words to the students were punctuated with tears. I never miss days at school. Now I would have to miss months of school.

Chemotherapy began for me on October 14. My dear mother, whose health had been seriously declining, died on October 16. Her funeral was October 19. Radiation therapy began for me on October 25. I would soon realize that when cancer attacks, the patient is not in a battle; rather, the patient is in a war.

The tumor began to shrink. The treatments were having an impact, yet the side effects of the treatments began to take a brutal toll. I lost 20 percent of my weight, and I was already thin. I became dehydrated. I could not swallow. Ten days in the hospital found me fighting cancer, the side effects of treatments, pneumonia, and a very serious infection. As I said to a pastor during the worst of those ten days, "I am at my limit. I cannot continue like this."

The students sent cards and letters. "Dr. Babbage, you are strong, you can beat this. Fight. Fight more. Keep fighting." A vast network was established to pray, pray more, keep praying. Finally, there was improvement as the pneumonia cleared up, the infection was cured, and the interrupted cancer treatments could begin anew.

My incentive was to return to teaching. I visited my political science class in late January to see if I could still teach. I tried that again in February. Yes, the students and I can still learn together. Cancer has not taken my teaching skills or my teaching enthusiasm.

February 28 I was blessed with the sufficient health to begin a week of teaching half days. It was invigorating. It was productive. It was therapeutic. It was a blessing. The next week was full-time teaching, and that continued until our seniors graduated on June 4.

A few days after graduation, with all end-of-year duties completed at school, I participated in an interview at the Kentucky Educational Television studios in Lexington. The topic was my war against cancer.

The interview gave me an opportunity to think of the life lessons that are learned when you battle a life-threatening disease. One lesson is the importance of an attitude that says, "I will survive this." That attitude gives you a reason to endure and a hope to prevail.

In some ways, top-down, bureaucratic, political, imposed reform of education is a disease, which the real work of education must survive. Top-down reform of education does not work, as evidenced by each top-down reform of education being followed by yet another top-down reform of education.

Thankfully, determined people enable the real work of education to survive despite the complications and counterproductive tendencies of top-down reforms. What really works in education and how everyone can support what really works in education are the areas of emphasis in this book. Learning in school will survive because grassroots efforts continue to provide answers to school improvements. That survival attitude energizes the grassroots efforts and the people who champion them.

Keen Babbage
June 2011
Lexington, Kentucky

Acknowledgments

Thank you to Henry Welles for encouraging me to write another book. Henry is a good friend from the college years. I was a freshman dormitory resident assistant in 1974–75, and Henry lived on the dormitory floor that I helped supervise. Henry, his wife, and family have lived in Austin, Texas, for many years. Henry and I keep in touch via letters, which are written and mailed through the postal system. It is a glorious tradition, and it is a traditionally honored method of communication.

Henry suggested that a book about how communities value, appreciate, and support teachers would be useful. From that splendid idea emerged this book and the inspiration to keep writing.

Cindy Henderson's word processing magic turns my handwritten words on notebook paper into proper computer type on the screen and then on the disk. She and her family have encouraged me to write, write more, and keep writing throughout the past eighteen years and throughout the fourteen books we have worked on together.

My brother Bob, sister-in-law Laura, niece Julie, and nephews Robert and Brian are always excited about "Uncle Keen's new book." Their support is essential.

The students I have taught at Henry Clay High School during 2006 through 2011 have shown me, as have other students for twenty-two prior years, that what matters most in education is what happens in the classroom to cause leaning.

Bill Goodman hosts several programs for Kentucky Educational Television. His encouraging e-mails during my cancer ordeal's worst times (2010–11) were so helpful. His interest in my cancer story led to a wonderful interview we did for his *One to One* program in June 2011. During that interview, he mentioned my book *The Dream and the Reality of Teaching*. He encouraged me to keep writing books. That encouragement ignited the renewed energy that helped create this book.

Please note my career experience in education includes twenty-seven years as a middle school and high school teacher and administrator. I have also taught graduate school. I have not worked in an elementary school, but I trust that elementary school educators can apply the ideas in this book with the necessary adjustments based on the unique needs of elementary school students.

As always, names and situations in this book are fictional; however, the ideas, issues, and circumstances are realistic.

This book is dedicated to my immediate family. My parents, Bob Babbage Sr. and Judy Babbage, took education seriously. They made sure that I did well in school. Our home was a place where education was valued, reading was required, lively conversations were constant, and faith was lived by example.

My maternal grandparents, Keen and Eunice Johnson, set timeless examples of honor, integrity, devotion, love, and faith. They made possible for me much of what I have been given and much of what I have achieved.

My brother and sister-in-law, Bob Babbage Jr. and Laura Babbage, plus their children—Robert, Julie, and Brian—are gems. They nursed me through my war against cancer in 2010 and 2011. They inspire many people, including me.

1

Everyone

"The teacher I am nominating is the best teacher I ever had. Middle school was a difficult time for me. I never made the school basketball team. Friends from elementary school seemed to turn against me for no reason. But there was Mr. Jefferson who taught me in seventh-grade science and then in eighth-grade math. He just never gave up on me. He was always available when I needed extra help with science or math. He knew I was really interested in cars, so he let me do a lot of science projects about how cars work. He even found math problems about cars so I could learn math and see why it mattered to me. He started a soccer team and encouraged me to participate."

"I went on to play high school soccer, and Mr. Jefferson came to some of my games every year I was in high school. So, Mr. Jefferson deserves this outstanding teacher award because he is the person who helped me the most. Because of what Mr. Jefferson did for me, I have a college scholarship to study engineering. I hope to design cars someday."

"The most important teacher for me is Ms. Sullivan. She taught me how to read. I really struggled with letters, with words, with sentences. All of the other students in second grade seemed to be reading with no difficulty. They did great on our spelling tests. I could not read much, and my spelling was awful. Then Ms. Sullivan spent some extra time with me. She had these old flash cards to help me identify words, define words, spell words. For some reason, something as simple as old-fashioned flash cards got something in my seven-year-old brain to work better than ever. By the time second grade was halfway through, I could read at third-grade level."

"Ms. Sullivan knew I was very interested in dancing. I started taking dance lessons when I was four years old, and I've been involved with dance, including ballet, since then. For a second grader to get to read books about dance, dancers, dancing made me eager to read. Ms. Sullivan helped me create a book about my early childhood experiences with dancing. I got to read that book to my class. They cheered and cheered for me. Ms. Sullivan gave me everything I needed to succeed in school. Next year I will be a college freshman because ten years ago Ms. Sullivan refused to let anything keep me from learning to read."

"Mr. Johnson is the best teacher I ever had. I was a sophomore in high school, and I had done average work in my ninth-grade year. My real interest was the band at school, especially marching band. I worked really hard at band camp, at band practices after school, and in band class. Music meant something to me. The other classes were just what I had to get through so someday I could finish high school and do what I really care about, which is to be a professional musician. Mr. Johnson watched one of our marching band practices one day after school. He was probably busy that day, but he took the time to watch us."

"A few days later, I got a test paper back from Mr. Johnson, and he had written this on it: 'You passed this test with a 71% grade. What happens in band if you play 71% of the notes correctly or if you step in the right place with the marching band program 71% of the time? Would 71% be acceptable for band performances? Don't you seek to play 100% of the notes correctly and to march in step 100% of the time? I've heard you play trumpet. I've seen you march. You expect yourself to be 100% right. Now, do the same thing in our world history class. Require yourself to be 100% ready for class, 100% attentive in class, 100% involved in class, and 100% successful in class. You and I both know that you can do that.'"

"Mr. Johnson was right. I had never thought about school the way I thought about music. That changed, not immediately but pretty fast. My average grades moved up to B or A grades in all classes. I once told Mr. Johnson that he had done brain surgery on me. I can't thank him enough. My career goal now is to be a high school music teacher and marching band director. Thanks, Mr. Johnson."

When high school seniors are given a chance to nominate teachers for awards, the statements the students make about the teachers are similar to those comments about Mr. Jefferson, Ms. Sullivan, and Mr. Johnson. The school district where I work does have a program that enables high school seniors to publicly pay tribute to their best teachers.

The comments the students share with the audience always refer to a teacher who "never gave up on me," "never let me do less than my best," "who took the time to be sure I learned even when I needed lots of help and probably did not appreciate everything being done for me," "cared about me, always encouraged me, came to the school events I was involved in." These comments help confirm what works best in education.

There is never a time when a high school senior says, "I know we are supposed to nominate a teacher, but I would like to nominate a law. The TEST law, it stands for Tomorrow's Education Starts Today, changed everything for me. From that law, I got to take class after class where everything we did came in prepackaged, detailed, scheduled programs. Every day in every class from eighth grade on was completely predictable because the TEST law told teachers exactly what to do, when to do it, and how to do it. Factories are not as efficient as our classes were."

"Of course, it meant we never did anything more challenging or more important or more useful than the TEST materials provided, but that was the price for what the state political leaders called accountability, efficiency, and productivity. TEST is a one-size-fits-all plan. It made school very simple and manageable. College will not be like that. My career will not be like that. Life will not be like that. But the education experts decided what every teacher and every student should do. I wish they had asked teachers and students. Still, I will graduate soon, so I guess it worked out. Thank you TEST for getting a high school diploma for me. I have one question—what does this diploma mean?"

Where and how do top-down, bureaucratic, political education reforms such as TEST originate and get approved? One possibility is that a candidate for governor of a state promises to be the education governor if she is elected. "For too long our schools have underachieved. We have some excellent schools, but we have so many schools that are ordinary or failing. Students today need an education that prepares them for the twenty-first-century challenges of tomorrow. We cannot hope that every student in every classroom gets a good education. We have to make sure that every student in every classroom gets a good education."

"I propose a systemic reform in this state. Our goal is to make the educational experience in each first-grade class outstanding and identical to the educational experience in every first-grade class. The same will be true for all grades and all subjects. The two thousand first-grade teachers in this state should not use two thousand different systems and methods of teaching. We will identify the best teaching system and method. We will then have every teacher use that best teaching system and method. My plan is called 'Tomorrow's Education Starts Today,' or 'TEST' for short."

What are the goals of this candidate for governor? To win the election and to improve schools. What does TEST have to do with these goals? It sounds good because it implies that one uniform system of teaching can be identified as the best system and can be imposed on each classroom. If this candidate for governor wins the election, she would work through laws, regulations, and policies to implement TEST. What might be gained in systemic, bureaucratic, political, regulatory uniformity would be matched or exceeded in what would be lost due to ignoring the classroom reality that education is not a systemic, political, regulatory process.

Education is a human adventure that must be allowed to vary as human needs, abilities, achievements, skills, personalities, and goals vary. One-size education does not fit all students; therefore, one method of education will not cause every student to learn.

What could the candidate for governor do instead of take some political consultant's advice that voters respond to promises to restructure, reform, and systemically correct education?

The candidate could recall the brilliance of Abraham Lincoln, who spoke of "government of the people, by the people, and for the people." The candidate for governor could listen to the people who know about schools, who care about schools, who pay the taxes for schools, who hire the graduates of schools, who work at schools, and who are impacted by schools.

The candidate for governor could hold a public forum, a town hall meeting, and listen to people express their ideas for and concerns about education. What could be heard at this town hall meeting? Consider the following samples of citizen input at a town hall meeting:

Candidate: I would like to thank everyone for being here today. As you know our topic is education. I am eager to listen to your thoughts on this topic. Our state must improve the results we get in education, but we need to do that in the ways that work best. We do not need to pass education laws that are impossible to implement because they are out of touch with reality even if they sound good or get applause. So, I am eager to hear your ideas, your concerns, and your suggestions.

Parent: I think the students need more of that old-fashioned memorizing. They need to know the multiplication table up to twelve. I taught that to my children, but their teacher said it was not emphasized because anyone could use a calculator to do multiplication. Well, I think something good happens in the brain when a student learns the multiplication table.

It's the same with spelling. What happened to those every Friday spelling tests in elementary school? I know. Computers can check spelling for you, but knowing how to spell is just part of being educated. If you can't multiply and you can't spell, you are missing some really important mental exercise and life skills.

One other thing concerns me. When I visit schools, I wonder why most of the teachers dress so casually. I go to my son's high school to visit classes once a month. I am very involved—my son probably thinks I am too involved—but to know what is going on at school you have to be there. I go to his football games, so I'm not going to let him think that I see football as more important than classes.

When I visit the school, it seems that teachers are dressed for a casual Saturday social event. Some students dress very casually, but the teachers need to set a professional standard in everything they do. If you want the students to look up to you, give them every possible reason to do that.

Guardian: I have legal guardianship of my two grandchildren. One is in eighth grade, and one is in eleventh grade. It has been a long time since I was in school. What they do now is different from what we did as students. Computers are everywhere in the school, and every student seems to have a cell phone, which they try to use all day long, at least that is what I hear. Anyway, my concern is reading. Do students still check out books from the school library, read them, and turn in a report on them? Isn't it still important to read real books?

I take my grandchildren to the public library once each month. All of us check out a book or two. We read at home. We talk about those books. Sometimes we all read the same book and discuss it. We have great discussions. I'm concerned that, as everything in society and in school becomes electronic or technological, reading books will be ancient history. Please make sure that reading books is emphasized in our schools.

Community leader: I represent an alliance of neighborhood groups in our county. We trade ideas about everything from neighborhood watch groups to recreational facilities. The topic of schools is frequently on our agenda because any neighborhood that has a school in it is impacted by the school—everything from traffic going to or coming from the school, to events at the school in the evening, which are open to the public, to possible community use of school buildings on weekends or in the summer. These are topics, among others, that we discuss.

Here's my thought. School buildings that are old need help. Do we have plans in our state to update or upgrade or renovate old school buildings? When a new school is built, it has everything up-to-date, but the old buildings just get further behind. Neighborhoods with a new building really benefit. The people are proud of their new school. Neighborhoods with the old schools still want what is best for the students, but the money goes to the new school, not to update every school. That just seems unfair to me and to many people I work with.

Reporter: I work for a newspaper, but I am not here tonight to write a story about this town hall meeting. I am here on my time to offer an idea. It really bothers me that most of the news we report about high schools deals with sports. The schools call us with sports news. The schools' athletic teams have websites filled with statistics, pictures, data, schedules, quotes that we can use. If a student can put a basketball through a hoop, we find out about it.

For the students whose skill is to perfectly translate Latin or to precisely do calculus problems or to have perfect attendance or to always make great grades, we are rarely told about that, and we rarely make an effort to get much information like that.

For people whose perception of our high schools is based on what they read in the newspaper, that perception leans toward high schools being the training grounds for future college athletes. I would like for newspaper stories about academic achievement of students to be more plentiful and more prominent than are the stores about athletic accomplishments. Sure, people are interested in sports, and there is a lot of good done for students through their participation in high school sports, but what really matters in school is what students learn. So I hope that schools and the media can do much more to present the full picture of what is happening at school.

Elected official: I am a school board member in Thompson County. I was elected originally seven years ago, and I was reelected three years ago. It takes a lot of time to attend the meetings and to keep informed, but it is important to me that I contribute to the community. Here's my topic. Testing. The state requires more testing in our schools than ever before. The principals and teachers tell me that, with all of the required tests for math, for reading, and for the annual comprehensive assessment, it takes eight full school days to complete all of the testing. Is that really the best use of those eight school days?

Then the national government keeps asking for more data about schools. So some more testing might be necessary. I'm sure that some testing can be helpful, but we are adding more testing every year, and I doubt that we need all of it. Then the tests change every few years, and it is hard to get a feel for what is happening long term if the tests keep changing.

I think the grades that teachers give tell a lot, in some ways tell more than a lot of those expensive, fancy tests tell. Grades are based on what students do day-to-day. A good teacher knows the students better than any one-day or eight-day test process knows the students. It seems to me that, instead of spending so much time and money on the tests we buy, we should have more thorough evaluation data on every student from the grades the student is earning day after day, week after week.

I know some people are concerned about grade inflation or about students who do little work and then pass a class with a lot of extra credit points. Well, a school can set up a policy about grading that the people at the school agree to and follow. It could limit or eliminate extra credit, if that is helpful. So, I would like to suggest that we do not need all of these expensive, time-consuming tests if our teachers are actually measuring student achievement with grades.

Taxpayer: I guess you could call me the typical citizen. I vote. I pay taxes. My husband and I send our three children to public school. We have a fifth-grade daughter, a seventh-grade son, and an eleventh-grade son. They are doing very well in school. My concern is this achievement gap we keep hearing about.

As I understand it, we take test scores for one group of students and see how those scores match up with the scores another group of students got. It might be girls versus boys or students on free lunch versus students who pay for lunch, or it could be based on ethnic group or on special education versus other education. So there is one number calculated for each group, and if the group numbers are not identical, someone complains about the achievement gap.

Now, think about this. In each group, there is a range of achievement. Some students in each group are doing better than other students in the same group. Squeezing all of that range into one statistic does not tell us about anyone. It creates some group number, but teachers do not teach those groups one group at a time. They teach classes of students, and each class could have several groups, but they give a grade to each individual. They do not give grades to a group of students based on the average of the grade each student in that group earned.

So, as a taxpayer, I think we are wasting a lot of time and a lot of money on these achievement gap calculations and the actions that follow. There is only one achievement gap that matters, and that is the gap between what a student is doing today and what that student is capable of doing.

We can work on that individual student's achievement gap. The way it is usually done assumes that all students in any underachieving group need some kind of help to bring them up to the better achieving group. That is not reality. The underachieving group could have some individuals who are doing superior work, but that does not show up when these scores get averaged with the rest of their gender, income, ethnic, or other groups.

The achievement gap strikes me as a politically correct initiative of the education bureaucracy to create lots of data, charts, meetings, programs, and accusations. Let's direct our time and effort to resolving each individual student's achievement gap between his or her current work and what he or she is capable of.

State government education official: There are 137 school districts in this state. No matter what the state government tells the school districts to do, unless it is a law with penalties for noncompliance, the 137 school districts do everything in 137 different ways. How can the state's education department provide the legislature and the governor the reports you need, the measurements you need, the data you need, and the accountability statistics you need if we have 137 variables in every collection of information we provide to legislators and to the executive office of the governor?

I know the school-district people and the school-level educators think that the state department of education is just one big bureaucracy where we sit in offices and attend meetings all day while the people in schools do the most important work. Well, our work is important also. I have visited most school districts in this state. You would be shocked at the range of quality from the best school to the worst school. There is no reason for such a wide range.

We know what the best states, the highest-ranked states for education, are doing. We just need to borrow their state education model and impose it on all of our school districts. If we do anything less than that, we guarantee that some of our school districts will succeed on their own and other school districts will fail on their own. Most teachers do not know what other teachers are doing well that could work for them. Most principals do not know what other principals are doing well that could work for them.

Only the state has the broad perspective to know what is working or is not working throughout the state and around the nation. I ask that you work to empower the state department of education to establish more uniformity across all of our 137 school districts. To do anything else is to maintain the undesirable range of the status quo.

Business owner: For many years, I have employed high school students to work at the movie theaters I own. I am always amazed at how serious and conscientious some of the teenagers are and how lazy and irresponsible some of the other teenagers are. What explains the difference? Grades.

I check on their grades because they have to show me their report cards. The students who make good grades are the best employees. They work hard, and I can count on them. The students who make low grades at school are the worst employees. They don't want to work, but they expect to get paid. They eventually quit, or I fire them.

My questions are what went right with the good students, what went wrong with the unsuccessful students, and what can schools do to get those failing students to improve? I am willing to help. I'll be glad to hire students who bring grades up and who quit getting in trouble. I'll be glad to hire honor-roll students and to pay them more.

Let's find ways to team up because schools need their students to learn well and I need my employees to work responsibly. We both want the same thing; plus, all of that can be very good for students.

Business manager: I go to several high schools in the region where I live and work. I go to recruit part-time employees who are juniors or seniors in high school. What concerns me is as I walk through the halls of the high school, I hear the most vulgar language from students; plus, most of the students are listening to some music device or are on their cell phones. Aren't there rules against this stuff?

The students I hire are told that being polite to customers and to other workers is required. No vulgar language. No casual, sloppy clothes. No listening to music at work, and no use of cell phones at work when you are on the company clock. These requirements are a shock to some of the teenagers. So I wonder if schools are teaching students what is required in the work world.

Former teacher: I was a teacher for thirty-three years. I get asked a lot if very much changed during all of those years, especially if students now are different from students years ago. I don't think so. Throughout my thirty-three years, most students cooperated and did their work most of the time.

What did change every five years or ten years or so was some big reform of education. We would be told that new laws required lots of changes in what we taught, in how we taught, and in how students would be evaluated with some new testing process.

Well, I saw five or six of these big education reforms. One would come and go; then the next would come and go. People in politics apparently thought they were experts on education, so they would pass the new and improved laws to finally solve all of the problems in the schools. The real problem was that these reforms never solved the real problems of school.

I don't know where people in politics get their ideas about what is going on in schools or about what schools need or about how to improve schools, but they never asked me or any other teachers to my knowledge. How are you going to improve schools if you do not talk to teachers? Who knows schools better than teachers? If you are so concerned about students, then talk to the teachers because they are with students every day, in every class, at every school.

Quit listening to those expensive consultants who come in to offer expensive advice to state government or to school boards. Teachers can give you better advice at no charge. So can principals.

Former principal: One of my concerns for people who make laws or regulations or policies about school is that you spend almost no time in schools. You pass laws telling educators how to educate students, but the truth is you could not come do the job you are telling us how to do. Schools should be all about educating each and every student, not about doing the paperwork that shows we are following the new, pointless requirements of the newest, most pointless bureaucratic procedures that do nothing for education but that do a lot of damage to education.

Here's an example. The state government thinks every student in kindergarten through high school should get thirty minutes of exercise daily at school. Who will teach that? Where will this exercise happen? Is the school gym available for this, or is each classroom going to become an exercise facility? Will the school day be extended by thirty minutes, or does the instructional program lose thirty minutes daily?

Exercise for students is good, but can't they do this exercise on their own after the school day? Can't their families be responsible for this? Schools are designed to educate students, not to deal with every emotional, social, physical, or other need that people aged five to eighteen have.

Current teacher: I love to teach. I look forward to each new school year. I never count down days in May as the end of the school year approaches. I am getting concerned about something. Years ago, the elementary schools were told to put less emphasis on spelling, math computation, and other basic skills. We have paid the price for that change. My middle school students are perplexed when I tell them that spelling counts. Our math teachers are stunned with how few math skills the students have. They can use a calculator, but they don't understand what addition is or what multiplication is.

I suggest that we emphasize the basic skills in elementary schools and in middle schools. Let's quit chasing every new trend in education, and let's not follow every new fad in education. Reading, writing, and arithmetic are still important and always will be no matter how electronic- or technology-based our society becomes. I bet the people who create all of the new electronic devices know how to read, write, and do math.

Speaking of technology, schools cannot keep up with every new invention. We spent a fortune on putting computers in classrooms and in computer labs. Now some people tell us that the personal computer is becoming obsolete. We do not have the funds or the personnel or the mechanical flexibility to change our machinery to match every innovation in technology. Sure, we need to use technology, but we can't be state-of-the-art in technology in every school when what is state-of-the-art in technology changes so often.

Current counselor: I am a high school counselor. I cry most days at school because I increasingly deal with heart-breaking situations that our students are involved in. The death of a parent. A student on drugs. A student who plans to drop out of school. A student who speaks of suicide after his best friend did commit suicide. A student whose single mother is now in jail. A student whose family was evicted from their apartment and has no home. Those students whose grandparents are their guardians. Students who are court involved for the crime they were found guilty of.

Our society tells us to deal with all of this. We do our best. I have little time to advise students about college or vocational school or the armed forces or careers because the emergencies of each day demand immediate attention. If our society is going to tell schools to do more, then society needs to do more for schools.

Current principal: My concern is that in education we make everything too complex, too complicated, too bureaucratic, too regimented. I talk to principals and to superintendents who tell me that more and more of their time is spent on politics, on budget battles, on real or threatened lawsuits, on implementing new regulations, on endless paperwork, and on similar time-consuming tasks when what they should work on is education. You know—students and teaching and learning.

I would ask everyone in state government and every school board member and every central office worker to have a one-year moratorium on new laws, policies, and regulations. Do not give us any new paperwork to do or procedures to follow. Let us take one year and make it all about students, teaching, and learning. I predict that the results would be so good that the moratorium would be extended for a second year.

We cannot regulate ourselves into education perfection, but with a total emphasis on students, teaching, and learning, we would get better results than any political reform of schools could ever get. Please, let schools be schools, let teachers be teachers, let principals be the principal teacher they once were—or instructional leader, to use the current term—and then students will have the academic achievement we all say is our highest priority.

Community member: I have listened closely to everyone. It is amazing how different the concerns are and how different the goals are. No wonder schools are less productive than they could be. Schools are filled with people who have vastly different ideas about what schools should accomplish. Schools are surrounded by communities that have vastly different ideas about what schools should accomplish. We are moving in so many different directions that, in attempting to do everything, we end up accomplishing less than we could.

Everyone at school is busy, but not everyone at school is moving in the same direction. I would suggest that schools need to have one singular, clear, certain dominant reason for being and that every decision, every action must be consistent with that one clear purpose. I have always thought that the purpose of a school is to cause learning. If every decision, every action is done to support learning, schools would achieve more and get distracted less by unnecessary activities.

Candidate: It truly has been fascinating to listen closely to every comment today. There is much to think about as we consider what needs to be done to improve education in our state. My campaign staff and I have analyzed some very promising education reforms from other states, but our goal is that the best education anywhere in the nation will happen right here in our state.

So, we could borrow some ideas from other states, and we could add many of our own ideas that you provided and that other people in our state offer. I will soon publish my education plan for our state, and I will be eager to read your comments on it, so please contact my campaign website to share your evaluation of the plan I will propose soon. Thank you for being here today.

The people who spoke at this town hall meeting had many varying ideas for and priorities for education. Is it practical to expect one school to successfully address every concern that was presented at the town hall meeting? Is there a better way to improve education than a broadly scattered approach that seeks to solve countless problems, large and small, educational and social, new and old?

Is there a better way to improve education than yet another top-down reform from a candidate for governor who gets elected, who gets the reform approved with some changes by the legislature, and who then expects every educator in the state to perfectly implement the reform whether it will help education or not?

There is a better way. For years, in the 1960s, 1970s, and beyond, Dr. Earl Reum taught high school student leaders that "people support what they help create." Top-down education reform ignores and violates that leadership and management aphorism. For education reform to have the desired impact of improving student achievement, the reform must enhance the work that teachers and students do in classrooms. It makes sense to include input from people who work in classrooms if the goal is to improve results in classrooms.

It also makes sense to work with all individuals and groups who are involved with, effected by, concerned about, and potentially helpful with education if the most school improvement is to occur.

It makes further sense if teachers, students, principals, counselors, superintendents, central office staff, school board members, community groups, parents, guardians, taxpayers, businesses, media, politicians, state government officials, and national government officials can agree on the purpose of a school. From the foundation of a shared purpose, real school improvement can be built. Through the filter of a shared school purpose, decisions can be made that support the school purpose, and actions can be taken that support the school purpose. Any decision or action contrary to the school purpose is not acceptable.

School purpose is much more than a mission statement. Mission statements are temporary. Mission statements are often vague. Mission statements are updated as new issues emerge or as the political winds change direction or as a new educational trend appears to be irresistible.

School purpose endures. School purpose is a statement of the fundamental reason that a school exists. School purpose is the standard through which all school decisions are made, all priorities are established, and all action that is contrary to the school purpose is rejected.

When a school district is selecting a new superintendent, when a school selects a new principal, when a teaching vacancy is filled, how is the best person chosen when many candidates bring impressive credentials? Evaluate the candidates in terms of who can do the most to fulfill the purpose of a school, which is to cause learning.

When six different textbooks are being considered for a middle school science class, select the book that will most effectively help the science teacher cause learning.

When a school is revising its discipline system, create the rules, the punishments, and the rewards that will most certainly cause students to learn right from wrong and the importance of selecting right instead of wrong.

When a community group brings a request to a high school asking that, at no cost to the school, a guest speaker affiliated with the community group be allowed to speak at the school, ask whether the content of the speech or the classroom instruction students would get by being in class is the better way to cause the learning that the school's curriculum obligates the school to singularly emphasize.

Every request from every community group to provide a guest speaker for a school may have merit, may be about an important topic, may be interesting and informative; however, all of those requests may need to be politely rejected because they do not most directly support and implement the school purpose. Even if those presentations cause learning, they may not most effectively cause the most important learning that the school's curriculum or the state's curriculum identifies as top priority.

Comprehensive commitment and adherence to a school purpose means that all decisions are made and all actions are taken in harmony throughout the school. There may be a faculty, staff, and administration of fifty, one hundred, or two hundred people at the school, yet they are unified in their work by the overall guidance that following a shared school purpose provides.

What is the difference between a school purpose and a shared school purpose? A shared school purpose is the result of consensus in its origin and is the result of each new employee knowing that everyone at this school fully commits to making all decisions and taking all actions consistent with the shared school purpose. There is room to be creative in how learning is caused. There is no room for creativity in wondering what today's school purpose is.

Am I causing learning? Am I causing the most learning? Am I causing the best learning? Am I causing the learning of this school's curriculum? Those questions can guide the work done by every educator and staff member at a school. If everyone can honestly answer "yes" to those questions, the school purpose can be implemented, and the desired results can be obtained. This effort would show the effectiveness of a grassroots school improvement.

This effort would be strengthened if everyone concerned about the school in particular and about education in general took only the actions and made only the decisions that support the purpose of a school in particular and the purpose of education in general—to cause learning.

"But I thought the purpose of a school was to prepare students for college or for their career or for the armed forces or for technical school."

"But I thought that schools were supposed to develop good citizens so students grow up to be responsible community members who work, pay taxes, support their families, vote, and do things like that."

"But I thought that, with so many changes in technology, schools were supposed to prepare students for jobs and challenges and opportunities of the twenty-first century."

Those three perspectives are reasonable. Those three goals could be included in an educational mission statement. Those three objectives all require that some very exact learning has to be caused. If the right learning is caused in the right ways and to the right depth, students are prepared for college, career, the armed forces, technical school, citizenship, community duties, and twenty-first-century technology; however, students are prepared for more than that.

Job descriptions change. Some jobs fade away as new jobs emerge. Education after high school could come in various ways and at multiple times throughout adult life. Technology is perpetually in motion as new products and systems replace last year's newest, best, fastest, most advanced product and system.

How can schools keep up with this relentless pace of change? By being 100 percent consistent in word and deed that the purpose of a school is to cause learning. Within that purpose is this: students will learn while they also learn how to learn; thus, they are prepared for unlimited learning throughout a lifetime.

The school purpose to cause learning does not have an expiration date. From kindergarten through high school, after thirteen years experiences of learning being caused, the student will know how to forever cause more learning.

Top-down education reforms are often based on good intentions but can also include other motives, such as a political agenda, a political career, community-group competition for status, self-serving intentions, desperation, search for power, bureaucratic manipulation, political-power turf wars, financial gain by consultants or vendors, and social engineering. Top-down education reforms assume that the people at the top know education best. By definition, this is inaccurate.

If you are at the top of the power pyramid or the education hierarchy, you do not know what is the day-to-day, minute-to-minute reality in classrooms, in school hallways, in school cafeterias, in school overall. You are not there. You could listen to and team up with the people who are there. You could listen to and team up with other people who care deeply about schools and who seek to impact schools. How such grassroots school improvement efforts can work will be detailed in the following chapters, beginning with the vital roles played by parents and guardians.

What became of the candidate for governor who hosted the town hall meeting? Let's consider two possibilities, and the reader can select the one that is better or can create a third option.

FIRST OPTION

It is with much hope and conviction that I propose my education plan for our state. These ideas are the best of the best. My public policy advisory board has compiled the most significant concepts from education reform efforts around the country and internationally. My plan is based on what is working best in other states and in other nations.

First, students need a longer school year—178 days is insufficient. I propose to add two days one year, five days in the second year, and ten days in the third year to increase our total to 195 instructional days. I purpose a reduction of seven days when teachers are at school but students are not at school. That will pay for the first increase of seven instructional days. The costs of the other ten additional instructional days would be shared by state government and local school boards with a new local revenue enhancement, which state government would match.

Second, the drop-out age will be increased to eighteen years; however, for any eighteen-year-old who does not graduate from high school, there would be no driver's license privilege. Also, employers could not hire anyone who dropped out unless that person was enrolled in an alternative graduation program.

Third, every student in every public school will have thirty minutes per day of physical exercise at school. The health and fitness trends for children and teenagers are alarming. Our schools can lead the way in reversing childhood and teenage health issues that have related to exercise and fitness.

Fourth, the typical pay system for teachers will change. The system says you make more money for each year of experience you complete and for each academic degree you add. Our new pay scale will put everyone at the same base salary rate and based on the results you get with your students, the more of a student achievement additive you will earn.

Fifth, far too many ninth-grade students fail many of their classes. This destines them to be at risk of continued failure. Each school district will create a new ninth-grade school building, reassign building usage to establish a ninth-grade center, or reconfigure how classrooms in high schools are used in order to create a school with a school.

Sixth, each principal, assistant principal, and central office personnel who are certified to teach will teach one class weekly or will substitute teach one full day per month. These people need to maintain awareness of and involvement in classroom realities.

Seventh, the grade of D will be eliminated. 75 percent will be the lowest C grade. We must increase the standards for our students.

One more part of my plan: school board meetings must be held at a school. The school could be different for each meeting in districts with many schools. School board members need to get out of their meeting location and into schools.

SECOND OPTION

I am prepared to announce my plan to improve education in our state. I propose a plan that will permit, in fact require, each school to solve its own problems and each school district to solve its own problems.

I have listened to much input from citizens of our state. I have listened to many educators. It is obvious to me that there are some outstanding teachers at every school. In every school district, there are some superior principals and assistant principals. These high-quality educators are getting results. State government should not tell these people what to do; rather, these people should work closely with their school colleagues and school district colleagues to trade success stories, to share great ideas, to answer each other's questions in a spirit of cooperation, of mutual learning, and of grassroots efforts to solve local problems plus to expand local successes.

My plan includes significant staff reductions at the state government's department of education. I visited that office complex for three full days. I saw endless meetings. I heard much office machine noise. What did all of that have to do with what really matters at schools? The staff positions at the state department of education that are not eliminated will be assigned to have direct contact daily with schools and school districts, including at least one day per week in the schools and school district the employee is the contact person for. The state education bureaucracy will change from going to meetings to going to schools to provide direct support.

One more part of my plan: I will instruct our state's attorney general to file a lawsuit challenging the national government's increasing involvement in education. The Tenth Amendment is clear, and education is a duty that belongs to the states and to the people. The national government's education bureaucracy is as bad as our state government's education bureaucracy. The U.S. Constitution gives the national government no authority in education. That is the way it should be.

If my plan seems to be the absence of a plan that is because this plan realizes that bureaucratic, political, top-down education reform never works. This plan trusts the people at the grass roots, in each school and in each school district, to create their future by improving their schools using the actions that will work at their schools for their students, for their educators, and for their communities.

This is democracy. This is logical. This is common sense. This is what works best because this plan liberates and empowers people to improve their schools by doing what their schools need, not by doing what the national and state governments tell them they need.

THIRD OPTION

One further thought about top-down educational reform that goes through the political process of the United States Congress and president or of a state legislature and governor—the resulting law will be the result of much compromise. The compromise process is fundamental to the political legislative procedures; however, laws that result from the compromise process may be a cut-and-paste collection of half ideas. One legislator seeks to mandate more testing to measure student performance. Another legislator seeks to reduce the amount of time and money allocated to mandated testing. A compromise is agreed to that increases testing at some grade levels and reduces testing at other grade levels. Is that plan the best way to test, or was it merely the politically possible plan that could get legislative and executive support?

When a teacher plans a lesson, the ideal is to create the lesson that best causes learning. The lesson is not a compromise with a few minutes of lecture, a few minutes of video, a short quiz, some group work, some reading, a quick use of technology, and an application to real life. That compromise includes so many pieces that confusion is more likely than learning. Top-down, politically mandated education reform does not work for many reasons, including the reality that political compromise does not create education precision.

2

Parents and Guardians

Show up, show up more, keep showing up. Be at school. Be at school more. Keep being at school.

Communicate with teachers, communicate more with teachers, keep communicating with teachers.

Ask questions of principals, of guidance counselors, of school board members, of central office personnel, of the superintendent, of Parent Teacher Association leaders, of state officials. Ask these questions politely with a sincere eagerness to know. Threats and confrontations are counterproductive.

Do not ask this question or other similar questions: "Well, it is January, and my son has failing grades. Why didn't you tell me?" It is your responsibility to know how your son is doing in school. The school probably sent report cards and progress reports. Your son's grade may be accessible to you via the Internet. The question in January about what you were not told, even if you were told it earlier, is avoided if you diligently monitor the work your son does or does not do and the grades he gets.

If you have a child who plays a high school sport, do you attend the games? Do you know the statistics of your son's performance in the sport? Are you paying as much attention to your son's academics as you are paying to your son's athletics?

If you have a daughter who is in the middle school band, do you attend band concerts more often than you visit her science class? If you have a son who is participating in an elementary school holiday musical performance, are you as likely to attend that as you are your son's presentation of a book report in his reading class?

The number of visits to school by parents and guardians seems to be largest in elementary school, with a decline in middle school and a continued decline in high school. The common reason could be that the older child or teenager would be uncomfortable if a parent or guardian attended class. Is that assumption valid? The seventeen-year-old football star does not tell his parents to miss his games because his friends would tease him if his parents were there. He will appreciate his parents being at the games. His friends will notice that. Those parents really support their son.

Now, show up in the United States history class or the calculus class, which the same seventeen-year-old is taking. By being there, you will know what the class is like. By being there, you can discuss the class with your son or daughter much more thoroughly. By being there, you show interest, concern, support, and encouragement. You also show that academics matter. If your time at school communicates the priority you give school, be there, and make sure you are there for academics more than anything else because academics matter more than anything else in education.

What improvement of school could be more grassroots than for a parent or guardian to be more involved in the educational experience of a son or daughter?

PARENTS AND GUARDIANS OF ELEMENTARY SCHOOL STUDENTS

The excitement that accompanies a five-year-old going to the first day of kindergarten is shared by the entire family. Pictures are taken. Plans are made. Many smiles are seen along with a few tears. The child could be taken to school by a parent or both parents, a guardian, or perhaps the extended family. This is a big event for the family as the day is anticipated, when the day arrives, and when the day is discussed. "How was your first day at school?" will be the major topic of family discussions when the young student has completed this day at school.

The first day of kindergarten has a unique excitement, which merits celebration. The seventy-second day of kindergarten is just as important as the first day was in terms of learning. On that seventy-second day, a skill could be worked on at school that absolutely must be mastered for continued academic success to be maximized. There is little or no celebration on the typical seventy-second day of kindergarten. There are probably no pictures taken as students enter the school on their seventy-second day of kindergarten.

There could be discussions at home after the seventy-second day of kindergarten. "How was your day at school? What did you learn? Show me what you worked on so we can find something at home that is similar and we can learn some more together."

What happens when a five-year-old kindergarten student has that discussion and that learning activity at home on the seventy-second day of kindergarten? Learning continues. Learning is encouraged. The priority of learning is reinforced. The experience of learning is shared. The idea that learning continues all day, every day is affirmed. The student more eagerly and more confidently returns to kindergarten tomorrow. The process is repeated on the seventy-third day of kindergarten, and the results are unlimited.

At the grassroots level of home and family, the school's purpose to cause learning can be continuously supported and daily experienced. The trip to a grocery store can be filled with a series of tasks or can be filled with a series of math problems, which accompany the tasks.

"You said that in kindergarten this week you worked on sizes and shapes, on larger than and smaller than. We need some cereal. Let's see what sizes the cereal boxes are and whether we need the size we always get or maybe one that is larger than that size or smaller than that size."

No education reform laws, policies, or regulations are needed to make that grocery store errand become an extension of kindergarten. Being aware of what the kindergarten student is learning and finding connections of that learning to everyday life is needed. Being aware requires much talking to the student, daily reading the teacher's website, knowing the kindergarten curriculum, and occasionally being in the kindergarten classroom to be more fully aware of the educational experience the student is having on a given day.

It is possible that a five-year-old whose family makes education a shared experience with a priority of causing learning continuously through shared family activities is a five-year-old whose educational foundation is more solid than any top-down reform of education could ever provide or imagine. If the family will continue this priority and these experiences, there could be a glorious day thirteen years later when this same student graduates from high school with superior results, with generous scholarships, and with ideal possibilities.

Two major factors in this family-based part of a grassroots approach to school improvement are time and interaction. Make, take, and invest the time with the five-year-old to create the interactions that cause learning. Turn off the television, turn off the computer, turn off the video game, turn off other electronic gadgets, and interact with each other face-to-face, mind to mind, brain to brain, person to person, parent/guardian to child.

"But I don't know how to teach my five-year-old about shapes. What am I supposed to do? What materials do I use?"

Look around your home. Is every item there the same shape? No, so select ten items, and have the five-year-old put them in groups that are shaped similarly. What basis did she use for the groups? What was similar about the items in each group? How did the items in the various groups differ? What are the correct names for each of the shapes? Then bring in ten more items to see if they fit in the existing groups or if another group might be needed.

The discussion about shapes can continue by going outdoors and seeing shapes in nature. The discussion can continue at supper by noticing shapes of different foods. The discussion can be continuous along with the learning by investing the time to create instructional interactions between parent/guardian and child. How many uses of your time and effort are more important? How many uses of your time and effort could create better memories?

Go to school. Go to school more. Keep going to school. Be at school often enough to know details about the education experiences your child is having and to be able to extend those educational experiences as you create family activities that apply to the kindergarten curriculum.

When you are at school, ask what you could do that would be helpful for the school, for the teachers, and for the students. Comply with any requirements to be approved as a school volunteer. Your volunteer involvement at school shows your child how important school is. Your involvement at school shows educators how much you appreciate and support their work. Your direct, personal, grassroots involvement at school helps make school a better place in ways that political, top-down education reform cannot achieve.

There is nothing complicated or sophisticated about a parent or guardian spending time at an elementary school. There is nothing complicated or sophisticated about a parent or guardian creating learning activities and interactions in the family home or as part of family events. The news media will not report on parents and guardians who visit school or who create learning moments at home.

Top-down, political, bureaucratic education reform endeavors, which rely on laws, regulations, and policies, are filled with complications and sophistication; however, time and effort invested by a parent or guardian in the elementary school education of a son or daughter will have a more direct, a more significant, a more meaningful, and a more lasting impact than the top-down approach can have. Parents and guardians can be part of a grassroots effort to improve schools, which accomplishes the desired result—to cause learning—through a complete dedication to cause learning.

The motives of top-down education reform may include learning but include much more, some of which is politics and social engineering rather than education. To the extent that parents and guardians help with the grassroots effort to cause learning, one student at a time, one classroom at a time, one school at a time, those parents and guardians help make a case that says that further top-down reform is not desired, needed, or to be tolerated.

PARENTS AND GUARDIANS OF MIDDLE SCHOOL STUDENTS

There are some teachers who would never consider teaching at the middle school level. There are other teachers who would consider only teaching at the middle school level. What explains the opposite perspectives on teaching middle school?

Some educators know that they are a good match with the unique needs and characteristics of elementary school students. They value the years they can spend with young children.

Some educators know that they are a good match with the unique needs and characteristics of high school students. They value the years they can spend with teenagers who are becoming young adults.

Other educators know that the only match for them is with the extremely unique needs and the extremely unique characteristics of middle school students. They value the years they can spend with older children who are entering the teenage part of life. The energy, the moods, the changing interests, the developing skills, the range of emotions, the endless curiosities of middle school students can be applied in the middle school classroom to help create energetic learning activities that work.

For parents and guardians of middle school students, there are very practical ways to support the educational experience of a son or daughter during these adolescent transition years. Be there. Be there more. Keep being there.

It is likely that very few parents or guardians of middle school students visit classes that their children take. Reasons may be as varied as the demands of a work schedule to the child who insists that it would be forever embarrassing if the parent or guardian attended middle school classes.

Work schedules can usually be adjusted or a vacation day can be taken or some employers may permit a parent to attend school for a few hours and make up that time later. Perhaps working overtime one day could create hours that can be used on another day to visit a school. An employer who supports education by helping employees attend school could benefit in many ways, including increased employee loyalty. Company policies can be written to provide clear and consistent procedures for this.

Perhaps the statement "I would be so embarrassed if you came to my classes" is a seventh grader's exaggerated way of saying "It might be ok, but please don't try to act cool." How the visit to school is experienced may determine the benefits.

Reasons to visit middle school include these: (1) middle school has changed since the parent or guardian was a student, (2) seeing and hearing what your child's classes are like is very revealing, (3) there is no substitute for being there if you want your child to know that you take something seriously, (4) you can acknowledge later at home the good work you heard and saw your child doing, and (5) as needed, you can make corrections or suggestions for what your child can improve.

Occasionally, a parent or guardian might tell a middle school child, "If your behavior does not improve at school and if your grades do not improve, I will come sit next to you and make sure everything improves." In some situations, that could be useful; however, before those problems arise, going to school could increase the success of the student in terms of behavior and of academics. Being there could prevent a problem, stop a problem at its beginning, or support and increase proper behavior and high-quality learning.

What can be done at home and with family activities to extend the learning and to connect with the learning that is caused at middle school? Begin by knowing the classes that are being taken and the content of those classes. A curriculum document for all parts of the middle school curriculum should be available at the school and/or via the Internet.

If the middle school curriculum includes United States history, a parent or guardian could identify some significant historical locations that are nearby and plan a family visit to the historical site. Perhaps a Civil War battlefield is a short drive away, and a reenactment of the battle will occur soon. Going to see that event can make your child the class expert on that topic.

Having books at home, purchased or from the public library, adds to the connection between school and home. Once you know the middle school curriculum, you can select books that match that content. Your son or daughter can be involved in selecting some books—the power of choice is potent.

Perhaps each of you read a different book about Thomas Jefferson, and then all of you evaluate for similarities and differences. Perhaps both of you read the same work of American literature, and then see how each of you react to the book. When some activities at home are designed to cause learning that the school's instructional activities are also designed to cause, the depth of knowledge is expanded, and the amount of learning increases.

Please notice, this school and home symbiosis can help reduce a perception from students that school is isolated from the rest of life and that school work is what has to be done before you get to do what is really important or interesting. Learning with your middle school son or daughter creates a different perspective by creating a shared experience based on the goal of causing learning.

The student may not wake up in the morning asking, "What is our family doing together today to cause learning?" Still, the student can find meaning, fascination, and learning in the activities that the family shares. When you visit that historical battlefield, you might stop at a pizza place on the way home for supper. A circular pizza cut into almost triangular slices is filled with arithmetic, algebra, and geometry questions, so make that supper another opportunity to cause family interaction, which simultaneously causes middle school math learning.

Middle school students are known to live in extremes. Today's best friend of your thirteen-year-old could be tomorrow's worst enemy of your thirteen-year-old, only to be the best friend again next week. A middle school guidance counselor can work with students who are having friendship troubles or who are starting rumors about each other or who are bullying. How can lessons in these areas be taught at home?

Your thirteen-year-old tells you that there is a new student in his science class. The new student just moved to your town from another state. Your child has lived in this town for his entire life. You and your son can discuss what it would be like to enter a new school without knowing anyone. You could list some friendly actions your son could take, such as having the new student eat lunch with your son and his friends.

Perhaps you could meet the family of the new student, welcome them to town, help them get settled, and set that friendship example for your son. Perhaps you work with your middle school's Parent Teacher Association and the school to be sure that every new family gets a sincere welcome, an orientation to the school and the community, plus contact names and phone numbers to use as questions come up.

The day could come when your usually obedient, polite, rule-following daughter gets in trouble at school. It is out of character for her, but the school official or teacher who calls to tell you is reporting the facts. The school will take discipline action. What will you do at home to cause additional learning, which the school's discipline action began?

If your daughter cheated on a test, your approach should not be to relentlessly look for an error in the school's investigation or to find another person to blame. Get the facts from the school officials or the teacher. Listen to your daughter's account. Help your daughter understand, again—she already knew—that cheating is wrong. Perhaps she was on the phone or the Internet last night so long that she did not study for a test. She and a friend she was on the phone with figured out a way to cheat.

There are many helpful lessons that a parent or guardian can teach in this situation and many proper ways to do that. The Internet and the phone could be off limits for some time. "The test grade is zero, but you will study for it, take it again, and keep taking it until you make an A." The daughter will make amends to the teacher by doing some responsible school service work. Your child will also have some additional duties at home to help teach the importance of honesty.

In some middle schools, the academic curriculum has created opportunities for seventh graders or eighth graders that previously were available only in high school. Taking geometry in middle school is an example. Participation in accelerated, gifted, and talented programs that lead to specialized high school programs is another example. Do not assume that what middle school students study now is identical to the classes you took in middle school.

Also do not assume that every middle school student takes the same classes as everyone else at the school. If there are accelerated programs or other unique experiences available at the school, find out about those and if they are beneficial for your child; then get your son or daughter enrolled in them. Of course, visit those classes or programs so you can create complementary learning causing experiences at home.

The middle school years can be the time for your son or daughter to have their first romance and heartbreak. This can also be the time when a thirteen-year-old gets curious about alcohol, other drugs, or some new mind-altering trend. Be alert; be very alert. If your home is drug free, it could help your child be drug free. If you secure all prescription and over-the-counter medications, that action can help prevent problems or tragedies. Find out what is taught in health class or science class at the middle school about relationships, alcohol, and other drugs, and continue the desired learning at home.

The middle school years can be a time of enjoyable exploration of proper curiosities. "Mom, I saw this movie at school, and I want to be an astronaut." "Dad, I just know I am going to own a business someday. We did this neat economy project at school today. Do we know anyone who owns a business and could tell me about it?" Explore those wholesome curiosities with your middle school son or daughter. The more wholesome curiosities you explore together, the less time or opportunity will be available for the thirteen-year-old to explore destructive curiosities.

PARENTS AND GUARDIANS OF HIGH SCHOOL STUDENTS

The usual trend is that parents and guardians are most involved with elementary schools, less involved with middle schools, and much less involved with high schools. There are common explanations for that predictable pattern, but there may not be convincing reasons. Is the high school experience of a son or daughter less important for a parent or guardian to be informed about and involved in than were the educational experiences of middle school or elementary school?

"But my sixteen-year-old would never forgive me if I visited her chemistry class or any class. She is struggling in chemistry class, and I think I could help her, but she would never be the same if I visited her class." If she is struggling in the class, you do not want her to remain the same.

Why does that same sixteen-year-old daughter love having her parents attend her soccer games but has somehow convinced those same parents that being in chemistry class is to be avoided? Who would be made more uncomfortable—the daughter or the parent—by a parental visit to the chemistry class? Why would there be any discomfort? If the parent has been in the habit throughout elementary, middle, and high school of visiting classes, then there is an established comfort level.

"But things just change in high school. It's not the same as when my daughter was younger. She is sixteen years old now. She is more mature and more responsible than when she was younger. She really does not need me to monitor her at school. I have to shift more of the responsibility of her education to her, don't I? Isn't that part of letting your child grow up?"

Wait a minute. Let's reconsider the just-stated assumption that the one reason a high school student's parent or guardian would go to school is to monitor the student. Visiting classes at the high school can create shared learning experiences that the parent and guardian can extend at home.

The high school curriculum now includes some classes that a generation ago or a decade ago were not taken until a student was in college. High school today is not identical to high school when a parent or guardian of a current high school student was in ninth through twelfth grades. Going to high school today for an occasional visit to one class or more classes can help today's parents and guardians more fully understand the opportunities, challenges, and realities of high school classes.

Be there. Be there more. Keep being there. The physics class you visit can become the basis of some exceptionally meaningful family activities and discussions. A family likes to bowl. The seventeen-year-old in that family dislikes physics class but loves bowling. Are there some applications of physics to bowling? Yes. Does the seventeen-year-old realize that knowledge of and application of physics could improve skills in bowling? A parent or guardian who visits physics class can extend that class to the next family bowling activity.

Does that seem to be simplistic? Does that seem to be too optimistic? Does that seem to be unrealistic given the busy schedules that all family members have? Are such questions like those more likely to be answered with excuses and rationalizations or with certain facts and realities?

The point is that the high school years can be incredibly productive, meaningful, and beneficial. It is possible that some high school students could guide themselves through high school in ways that maximize the learning experience, but that is unlikely. Even the most conscientious high school student is unlikely to be fully aware of every class that is offered, every detail about Advanced Placement classes, all of the procedures for taking dual credit classes at the high school, or for taking actual college classes prior to graduation from high school.

A parent or guardian can work with the student, a school counselor, and a school administrator to fully inform the student of every academic opportunity that the high school provides. Few entering ninth graders would otherwise know all of that or be ready to maximize the benefits of all of that without some initial and on-going adult guidance.

Imagine a parent who never took calculus but whose seventeen-year-old daughter is taking calculus. The daughter can be the family expert on this high-level math. The daughter could teach calculus to her mother. That could cause some wonderful learning of math and some wonderful mother and daughter learning about each other. No top-down education reform could duplicate that potentially precious grassroots, family-centered learning improvement.

The parent or guardian who occasionally or regularly visits high school will hear, see, and become aware of conditions at the school, which range from the very impressive to the very bothersome. Those observations, successes, and concerns can be reported to the school administrators.

"You need to know that Mr. Augustine is an outstanding teacher. I have visited his advanced Spanish class twice, and it is fantastic. He uses such a great variety of teaching methods, and he challenges all of his students all of the time." "The vulgar language in the hallways is crude, offensive, and everywhere. The other taxpayers of our community would be outraged as I am if they heard this verbal filth. How can the best possible learning take place in a building with the worst possible language everywhere you listen?"

The parent or guardian who participates in the grassroots effort to improve the academic achievement of a son or daughter is playing a vital role in overall school improvement. One family at a time, one parent or guardian at time, impacting one student at a time and investing more time and effort in causing learning will produce greater, more personal, more meaningful, more useful, more real, more worthwhile results than any top-down, political, and bureaucratic education reform can. Plus, the family efforts have a lasting quality and continuity while top-down reforms change, are replaced, and then the replacement is replaced.

A parent asks the sixteen-year-old high school sophomore, "Do you have any homework today?" The answer could be, "Not much. I got some done at school. I maybe have thirty minutes of math to do. That's it." What is the reply of the parent or guardian? Let's consider some possibilities:

1. "Ok. Be sure to get that done."
2. "Great. That means you can cut the grass today and finish cleaning the garage."

3. "Well, get some exercise. Maybe you can play tennis again at the park like you did last week. Then get that math done before supper. After supper you can read more of the Lincoln biography that you and I are reading."
4. "I checked the websites of your teachers. You have a World History test in two days and a chemistry test the day after that. Study for those tonight."

Homework. One version of homework, the more likely version, is academic work assigned by a teacher for students to do at home. To the extent that students take the homework assignments seriously, do the assignments completely, correctly, and on time, and do their own work, learning can be caused through the teacher-assigned homework.

Another version of homework, the less common version, is for a parent or guardian to assign academic work that the student will do and that the parent or guardian will also do or, at least will thoroughly discuss and think about with the student when the home-assigned homework is completed.

Some families of high school students will check with the school to find out if there is any required summer reading. If there is summer reading, the parent or guardian can work with the son or daughter to set up a summer reading schedule with specific reading amounts to be completed by certain days. The parent or guardian can also do the same summer reading to create family discussions, which cause learning by both generations.

Whether there is or is not a required summer reading assignment by the school, there can be a required and shared summer reading assignment assigned by the family. Maybe the student selects a book for the family to read, and the parent(s) or guardian(s) also selects another book for the family to read. Learning will be caused as the family reads, thinks, analyzes, and discusses together.

No new law is required to make this happen. No new regulation or policy is needed. No new tax has to be imposed. This is another example of how a family can cause learning in a grassroots, at-home activity, which leads to school improvements.

The high school student whose summer included reading and analyzing several interesting and challenging books is more prepared for school when the new school year begins. There can be plenty of time in the summer for a part-time job, for activities with friends, for a family vacation, for a church youth group mission trip, and for other wholesome summer experiences, in addition to reading.

"But isn't the school supposed to take care of all of that? I mean, the school is in charge of all the education stuff, right? I wouldn't know what to do for homework I assign at home."

Education is more productive when it is a shared responsibility and a shared experience. When a child or teenager is ill and the parent or guardian takes that young person to the doctor, there will be responsibilities that are carried out at home to implement the get-well instructions and plan that the physician provided. It would be illogical to claim, "Isn't it the doctor's responsibility to take care of all that medical stuff?" The doctor does have much responsibility, yet the parent or guardian and the patient have responsibilities also. To maximize education, a similar approach to shared responsibilities is helpful.

As a physician may prescribe medication, a school "prescribes" reading. There is no limit on learning for a person who will read, read more, keep reading. The family that makes reading a family priority will teach young children from very early ages that reading is essential. The adventure of reading then becomes a habit, a part of life almost as regular as meals. Food feeds the body, so the family makes sure that all family members are well fed. Books feed the brain, so the family makes sure that all family members' brains are well fed.

OVERALL IDEAS FOR PARENTS AND GUARDIANS

Think, please, of the role you are yourself playing in the education of your child. Are you fully informed, active, involved, and eagerly participating? Are you partially informed, occasionally active, sometimes involved, and rarely participating? Do you assume that, unless you hear from the school about a problem, everything must be going well?

Do you attend events at school, do you ask many questions, do you visit classes, do you know the teachers your child has every year, do you know the guidance counselors and the school administrators? Do you know the policies and the rules at school dealing with absences, make-up work, extracurricular activities, homework, and dress code? Is school only what the full-time professional educators provide, or is that experience extended, enhanced, and supported by what the full-time parent or guardian provides additionally?

The reality is that top-down, political, bureaucratic, systemic, "we will make our schools the best in the world" reform of education does not work. Every such reform falls short of what it promises and is followed by another top-down reform that falls short of what it promises. There is no elusive perfect top-down education reform because top-down reform is inherently imperfect.

Education happens at the grassroots level. Education at school happens primarily in classrooms. The classroom experience can be supported, extended, and enhanced by parents and guardians who see the education of their children as a responsibility that is shared with the school.

In addition to top-down reform not working, the national government and the state governments are, at the time this book is being written, faced with very difficult financial issues. The money that top-down political reform efforts costs is less available. Of course, since top-down reform does not work, why give such programs any money?

There is a patriotic and civic call to action going toward all parents and guardians—it is your duty and it can be your joy to be involved in the education of your children more than ever. Education is best provided as a shared responsibility, with parents and guardians deeply involved in the day-to-day learning experiences of their children. The following case study gives an example.

MOM AND DAD GO TO MIDDLE SCHOOL

"Mom, I give up. This assignment makes no sense. I don't know what people in 1787 were thinking when they wrote the Preamble to the Constitution. How am I supposed to analyze what it means? That was a long time ago. Who cares about things that are so old?"

"Well, Matthew, I think you can figure it out. Here, let me read the assignment and see if I can help explain it."

Matthew's mother read what the teacher had given to each student. "The Preamble to the United States Constitution is very beautifully written. It has many important and big ideas in it. Read the Preamble, and select the two most important ideas in it. Explain why those ideas were important in 1787, and explain why they are still important today." Mom had an idea.

"Matthew, make a list of the ideas in the Preamble. The list might make it easier to identify each idea than when you read the Preamble in its usual form. Then pick the two ideas that get your attention most. Tell why those two ideas stand out to you. Put yourself in 1787, and evaluate those two ideas. Then put yourself in today's time as an eighth grader, and evaluate those ideas."

Matthew was willing to follow his mother's advice, but he still was not excited about this assignment, and he still did not think that the assignment was worth all this effort.

Matthew decided that the most important ideas in the Preamble were (1) establish justice and (2) secure the blessings of liberty. His explanation included that everyone deserves to be treated fairly and everyone deserves to be free. He completed the assignment and showed it to his mother, who was quite impressed. Matthew's grade of A on the paper showed that his teacher was also impressed. Did that end this topic for Matthew? No, because his mother realized that there was more learning to be caused.

"Matthew, your father, your sister, you, and I are going to write a family preamble. You know, it would start with, 'We, the members of the O'Connell family in order to form a more perfect home life for everyone,' and then keep going. We each get to provide ideas, and we will all agree to the final wording. It might sound like school work, but it could mean a lot to us."

"Mom, that's a great idea. Let's be sure to include something about provide for the common dinner to include pizza once a week and stuff like that."

"Clever idea, Matthew, very creative thinking. You just might end up with a family preamble that guarantees your favorite supper each week."

"Great. This will be one writing assignment I can't wait to finish. The sooner we get a family preamble, the sooner I, make that we the people, get pizza for supper."

What will Matthew learn as his family writes their O'Connell Preamble? Preambles are as useful now as they have been for a long time. Work done for school can also have practical, personal, and desirable applications at home. School assignments do not necessarily end when they are turned in because the learning that the assignment started can be continued at home. Mom understands the work an eighth grader does more than Matthew realized.

Matthew told his eighth grade United States history teacher about the O'Connell Family Preamble. The teacher loved the idea. With permission of Mr. and Mrs. O'Connell, the teacher posted information about writing a family preamble on the school's website. The teacher, Mr. Lancaster, arranged for Mr. and Mrs. O'Connell to present their family preamble idea at the school's next PTA meeting. This led to the creation of a link on the school's website where parents, guardians, students, teachers, school counselors, and school administrators could post ideas that families could use to extend school assignments with closely related learning-causing activities at home.

Within a year, all of the middle schools in this school district had begun similar education-extension idea-sharing on their websites. This action got results efficiently. The requirements were not laws, taxes, bureaucracy, and procedures. The requirements were creativity, communication, time, and work. The purpose was to cause learning. The result was that learning was caused, families shared valuable conversations, and schools were improved.

If the case study about "Mom and Dad Go to Middle School" sounds optimistic, it is because educators must be optimistic. Working in a school is more demanding, more exhausting, more complex, more difficult, more frustrating, more fascinating, and more important than ever. Top-down political, bureaucratic, systemic reform is one reason for the increased difficulties, complexities, and frustrations.

When teachers can concentrate on teaching, when educators can concentrate on education, the rewards and the results of working at school increase.

When teachers can concentrate on teaching, when educators can concentrate on education—not on politics or on bureaucratic procedures—a much higher quality and much more quantity of learning is caused.

When parents and guardians regularly participate in the activities of education, the learning that is caused increases, perhaps multiplies.

It is as if a modern Paul Revere is warning, "The reforms are coming. The reforms are coming," but an all-inclusive school, family, and community grassroots alliance shows that the reforms are quite unnecessary. We the people at the grass roots are going to improve schools. In the next chapter, the emphasis will be how community groups can help cause learning and can help the grassroots effort to improve schools.

3

Community Groups

The purpose of a school is to cause learning. The learning to be caused is clearly identified in a curriculum document, a program of studies, a statement of standards, or a similar written plan.

The purpose of a community group's involvement in education is to help and to support a school or a group of schools in the effort to cause the intended learning.

The motive of a community group's involvement in education cannot be to promote its agenda, to boost the ego of its spokesman or spokeswoman, to score political points, to put in the news the name and face of its leader who anticipates a career move or a political campaign that will benefit from free publicity, and cannot be to stir up controversy. It would be better for community groups with motives such as those to stay out of discussions and actions that impact education.

A community group that is known for service projects may recruit members of the group to volunteer in school libraries to read with elementary school students. A community group of retired business leaders could provide guest speakers to high school business and economics classes.

A community group of people interested in local history could make presentations to middle school United States history classes. A community group interested in the environment could advise schools on recycling programs and other green initiatives.

Consider a community group known as the Students' Advocates for Education. The name sounds fairly positive and indicates that this group supports education for all students. On a closer look, the group has a very narrow concentration with stated concerns for only one group of students.

"Our organization is convinced that the discipline system in our schools is unfair to students who come from low income families. These students are suspended more from school and are expelled more from school than any other group. The school system, the school administrators, and the teachers obviously are discriminating. We will stand by, work with, and be with students in this group at any suspension hearing and at any expulsion hearing. Justice will be done."

There could be confidentiality limitations that prohibit nonfamily members of a student from attending such hearings. There could be legal, policy, or regulation language that states who may attend such hearings and who may not. The group may not have taken the time to learn about such procedures, but taking that time would be well advised.

How could this community group shift from being so adversarial to being more cooperative while maintaining a commitment to their concern about the discipline process? Rather than making the harsh accusations about injustice, the group could have some of its members volunteer to be on the school district's annual Discipline Policies and Procedures Review Committee.

Through this committee, there can be a thorough analysis of discipline statistics, of the discipline procedures, and of current rules and penalties for disobedience and input from students, teachers, school administrators, parents, and guardians. The goal of this committee would be to fully learn about the school system's discipline process and to offer ideas for improvement.

This approach avoids court cases, threats of court cases, confrontation, and headlines. This approach helps determine the real motive of the community group—is it to create tension and alarmist publicity, or is it to actually do the demanding work that leads to school improvement? Is the motive to get on the local television news with extreme accusations, or is it to cause learning about the facts of the discipline process?

When misbehavior occurs at a school, the teachers and school administrators must deal with it. The teachers and the school administrators do not invent misbehaviors. If a higher percentage of one group at school gets in trouble, the educators did not make those students misbehave. A thorough study of why all misbehaviors happen could be helpful. Within that overall study, some insights about particular groups could be found.

The goal, to be productive and useful for education, of the community group must be to improve education. The discipline system can be the way that some learning is caused for some students. The learning is about right and wrong rather than science or reading, but it is valuable learning. Supporting that learning is helpful. Disrupting or weakening that learning in the pursuit of questionable motives is destructive.

School budgets tend to be tight. The budget allocations need to reflect the priority of causing learning. Spend money on what most effectively causes the intended learning. Do not spend money on other requests for funds.

"But the campus is so plain looking. There is nothing that makes this school's campus inviting or impressive at first look. Is there no way to do some simple landscaping? I know we need textbooks and computers, but maybe if the campus looked more attractive, the students and everyone else at school plus the community would take more pride in the school."

How could a community group help with this landscaping question? "Our garden club is always looking for ways to beautify the community. We can get donations of plants and other supplies. Our members have all the equipment needed. We just need a landscape design or plan, and we can make this happen."

"Here's a possibility. My grandson and my granddaughter go to the elementary school in our neighborhood. We could work with teachers and students to make this landscaping project part of their science class. They study plants and weather and stuff like that. We could get a landscape designer to speak to a class or two, and the students could help create the plan. The campus will look great, and the students will learn a lot of science."

At the opposite end of the spectrum from the very supportive, helpful, and symbiotic work of the community garden club and the elementary school is a community group known as Ask Your Question. This group has a quarterly meeting open to the public where anyone can come and voice their complaint about anything or anyone associated with the local government, local businesses, local media, or local schools. Accusations, usually unfounded, are made. Names are named. Few people take the group seriously because they create much more noise than they create constructive ideas.

What would work better? The people who speak at the Ask Your Question meetings should ask themselves what their motives are, should evaluate their methods, and should raise their standards. A loud complaint at a public gathering creates animosity and battle lines. Going to school and meeting with educators in search of solutions creates partnerships. In their attempt to be noticed, some community groups overlook, perhaps intentionally, established methods and systems to address and solve problems at schools.

Please note, it is very beneficial to call ahead and schedule a time to meet with the teacher, school counselor, and/or school administrator. Just showing up at school and expecting the educators to stop what they are doing and meet with you is unrealistic and is impolite. How action is taken can be as important as the action itself.

The garden club effectively supported the school's purpose to cause learning. The Ask Your Question group shows no indication of interest in causing learning or in helping schools cause learning. The Ask Your Question group exists to loudly and publicly complain as if it were a radio talk show. How does an unfounded complaint followed up with no effort to reason together accomplish anything useful to improve a school?

Community disagreements should not be imposed on schools. Schools and school districts should not be places where community groups seek to fight their political battles. Consider the following case study.

GAP, REAL, AND THE SCHOOL SUPPORT NETWORK

"We are outraged by the achievement gap in this school district. The statistics are obvious. Some groups of students do well. Apparently, those higher-achieving student groups have been doing well for years. Other groups have average results while other groups are far behind. This is unacceptable and must be corrected now."

"We have formed a new group known as Gaining Academic Performance. You may call us 'GAP' because that is our priority, our concentration, and our issue."

"We will attend school board meetings and ask questions about what is being done to fix the achievement gap or gaps in our school district. We will attend meetings at schools and ask the same questions. We will keep the media informed, and we expect them to keep this issue in front of the community. We will vote. We will be heard. We will get results."

At about the same time, another community group was established. This group known as REAL, which stands for Rigorous Education Achieves Learning, also held a press conference similar to the GAP press conference, whose opening statement is quoted above. The REAL press conference began with a different opening statement with a tone and with content that showed another perspective.

"Our beginning goal is for every student, each student, one and all, to succeed academically. Our greater goal is for each student to excel academically. For this to happen, we suggest that some existing thinking needs to change."

"There is concern in this community and across the nation about the achievement gap. We are convinced that the achievement gap discussion to-date has been misleading because it is based on a questionable premise."

"The test scores of one group of students are averaged into one number, which is said to represent that group. Then the test scores of another group of students are averaged into one number, which is said to represent the second group. The two averaged numbers, for example, are 76 for group one and 85 for group two. The conclusion reached by some people is that a nine-point achievement gap exists; therefore, one group must have been discriminated against, one group was treated unfairly, one group was given fewer educational opportunities, one other group was given more educational opportunities."

"We have studied recent test scores that were the basis for some claims of an achievement gap at a local high school. The truth is that the lower performing group had some very high scores in it. In fact, five out of the top ten scores on the test came from five students in the lower achieving group. Typical achievement gap analysis could assign those five high achieving students to the same remedial work that everyone in the lower performing group will be required to do. How does that make sense? We conclude that it does not make sense and that discussions about the achievement gap thus far have created more confusion than they have created solutions. We offer another idea."

"First, let's apply the common achievement gap approach to other topics. A high school basketball coach notices that free-throw shooting on his team is not good. This is costing the team some games, which, with better free-throw shooting, could have become victories. The coach analyzes the statistics and finds some free-throw shooting gaps."

"Basketball team members who are high school juniors or seniors are hitting 61 percent of their free throws. The team members who are sophomores or freshmen are hitting 48 percent of their free throws. The conclusion is that all sophomores and freshmen on the team will spend fifteen minutes at each practice working on free throws until their group improves to 61 percent or better on free throws. The coach would prefer 70 percent for the entire team but has to get the gap group up first."

"One sophomore on the team has been hitting 72 percent of his free throws. One freshman has been hitting 74 percent of his free throws. One senior has been hitting 50 percent of his free throws, and one junior has hit only 43 percent of his free throws. Due to the number of people on the team in each grade level and the varying number of free throws each player has taken, the group statistic does not match the statistic for any one person in a group. It would be better to analyze the free-throw statistic for each player individually along with other statistics for each player to identify exactly what each person needs to work on to become a better basketball player. One player may need to work on free throws while another player needs extra work on three-point shots, yet another player needs to work making better shot selection."

"Now consider a fast food restaurant chain that has one thousand restaurant locations. The one thousand locations are ranked in terms of sales changes this year versus last year. In the top five hundred restaurants, sales increased 6 percent. In the bottom five hundred restaurants, sales increased 1 percent. There is a sales increase gap, but in the top group, there were some locations with a decrease in sales. In the bottom half, there were some locations with increases above 6 percent."

"This company will not get the best possible results if it imposes certain actions that all of the top five hundred stores must follow and a different set of actions that all of the bottom five hundred stores must follow. The competitive factors for all one thousand stores are different. The marketplaces are different. They may need one thousand unique restaurant improvement plans so the reality faced by each individual restaurant is addressed instead of the generic factors that the two groups of restaurants seem to face."

"We hope that our point is clear and is convincing. The perceptions of and the conclusions about the achievement gaps in our schools are faulty. The resulting actions directed toward those achievement gaps have been of limited impact because they were based on faulty perceptions and conclusions. There is a better way."

"Rigorous Education Achieves Learning. We understand that our school district is dedicated to the clear understanding that the purpose of a school is to cause learning. Our group hopes to cause learning about the achievement gap so each student benefits. The achievement gap we seek to close is the difference between what each student is achieving now and what each student can achieve. This means analyzing the grades of, the test scores of, and other data about each individual student. Then an individual plan is established for each student to maximize the learning for that individual student."

"We can close each individual's achievement gap through rigorous education, challenging educational experiences, meaningful educational experiences. When we close each individual student's achievement gap, we will have caused learning for everyone. That can be done. That must be done."

The two groups, GAP and REAL, continued to approach the achievement gap problem from their opposite perspectives and opposite ways of taking action.

GAP members attended meetings as they had promised. They attended school board meetings, school committee meetings, state government legislative committee meetings, state school board meetings, and meetings of professional education groups, such as the state association of principals and the state association of school counselors.

GAP members asked many questions as they had promised. Their questions usually had a tone of accusation and animosity. The answers they were given were direct, short, and often laced with much vague educational jargon and/or with an avalanche of overwhelming statistics.

GAP membership declined after a year, apparently due to the members finding it unproductive or inefficient to keep going to meetings. As one GAP member stated, "There are always more meetings to attend. I did not join this group to sit down in meetings. I intended to stand up for students."

REAL members had a different experience and saw different results. REAL's idea of closing each individual student's achievement gap was logical and convincing. Principals and teachers were eager to use that approach, but they asked a realistic question: "Where will principals, counselors, and teachers get the time to analyze the test scores, the grades, and other input about each student so an individual achievement growth plan can be created, implemented, and monitored for each student?"

The answer that found favor was for REAL members to become approved as substitute teachers and to do substitute teaching as volunteers. It was further agreed that the school district's central office personnel, including the superintendent plus the school board members, would substitute teach.

A schedule was set up so during the first and second months of school there would be enough volunteer substitute teachers at each school in the school district that sufficient time could be available for teachers to work with school counselors and school administrators to create the individual achievement growth plans. A similar schedule would be established in February to monitor each student's academic growth.

One unintended result of this plan was that the central office workers, superintendent, and school board members were given a new appreciation of and a more realistic understanding of the demands that are placed daily on classroom teachers. The REAL members had similar eye-opening experiences, and some decided to volunteer at school occasionally on days they did not substitute teach so they could do time-consuming tasks for teachers, such as make copies of materials or help create materials for upcoming projects.

Membership in REAL increased. A newspaper reporter wrote a very favorable article about REAL, and that attracted new participants. REAL won a community award for most productive new volunteer organization. Most students responded positively to their individual growth plan. Much learning was caused at school and about school.

School budgets are often tight and are likely to become more limited as local, state, and national governments deal with financial pressures. From 1981 through the following thirty years, this nation was financially irresponsible as the national debt increased from $1 trillion to $14 trillion. Many families and individuals increased their debt excessively during that time. Local and state government budget cuts can impact education and services that are related to education. How could a community group help schools during times of serious financial limitations? The following idea is one example.

When a company, a retail business, a restaurant, a bank, a not-for-profit organization, a charity, a church, or other group remodels or renovates its office, what is done with the old furniture? When a family downsizes from the house where they have lived for thirty-one years to a smaller "empty nest" home, what is done with the furniture and other items that no family member is going to use? When a governmental agency upgrades its computer system, what is done with the old computers?

The School Support Network would match groups that have a surplus of items, or that have items that are being replaced, with schools that could put those supplies to good use. The network's website is updated whenever a donating member of the network has anything useful to post on the website. Teachers, school administrators, school counselors, and school staff members can easily access the website. When items that can be used at a school are seen on the website, those items are claimed, and delivery is arranged. Everyone benefits.

The donating organization does not have to discard the items, and the school does not have to purchase the items. Why have a used file cabinet end up in the local landfill or at a garage sale when a school could put the file cabinet to good use? What a school does not have to purchase is something that tax dollars do not have to be spent on. This permits schools to allocate their budgets to the expenses that most directly support the causing of learning.

Another file cabinet in the school office is necessary, but an English literature book for a high school senior taking an advanced class or an algebra book for an eighth grader is essential. When the community can transfer assets, such as office furniture or used computers, from local organizations to local schools, everyone wins. This also shows the students and the educators how seriously the local community supports schools, and it shows that these are creative ways to solve budget problems.

In one community, a group of local artists began wondering what they could do to support art education in the schools in particular and what they could do to support education in general. Their brainstorming included making themselves available to work with local art teachers in the schools, perhaps to give individual guidance, instruction, or mentoring to a few students.

They knew of schools in other towns where students had designed and painted large murals on the school hallway and walls, and they were eager to help with similar projects. They thought of creating a Fine Arts Guest Bureau where local artists or musicians could be listed in a brochure along with a short biographical and career summary. Art and music teachers could use this brochure for information about guest speakers, guest artists, and guest performances for art and music classes.

The artists group was encouraged by one high school principal to create the guest bureau brochure. The idea grew. One musician from a local university suggested that university professors in many academic fields could be recruited for this new, expanding program. A chemistry professor could visit a high school chemistry class and begin to mentor future chemists, some of whom may be in her college chemistry classes in two or three years.

The results surpassed what the artists group had imagined. What was intended as a brochure became both a book and a website. Artists, musicians, university professors, business owners, political leaders, local authors, journalists, health experts, computer experts, automobile technicians, and many others made themselves available to schools to serve as guest speakers, mentors, and tutors.

Much learning was caused as students met these local experts, as teachers got new ideas about how to connect their subjects with the local community where the students live, and as the community members learned that the success of schools mattered more than ever to them because they were now actively involved in an effort to support that success.

The participants in the speakers' bureau donated the relatively few dollars that were needed to publish the book annually and to update the website often. A middle school yearbook staff was recruited to help with the book's annual update. Some high school students who were computer experts helped with the website. Much learning was caused and much more learning would be caused as this creative program continued.

The speakers' bureau involved no tax money. The speakers' bureau did not require a set of new laws from state government or local government. The speakers' bureau was not approved by, regulated by, or known to the national government. The speakers' bureau was not part of a top-down education reform program that mandated that every school district establish a policy for establishing a speakers' bureau and then begin a speakers' bureau within one year.

The speakers' bureau was a local effort, which was of, by, and for the local community. It was purely grassroots work to improve schools. It was people in a community working with educators in that community to make a direct difference for good in the schools. The results were great, and more great results will continue.

Unlike top-down, political, bureaucratic, mandated reforms of education, which are replaced in a few years as the political winds start to blow in a new direction, the speakers' bureau will endure and will continue to work. Why? Because the speakers' bureau helps to cause the learning that schools intended to cause. The same statement cannot be said of top-down, political, bureaucratic, systemic reforms of education.

"We think it is essential to the health of individuals, to the health of our nation, to the wise management of health care costs that children and teenagers get thirty minutes daily of vigorous physical exercise. We propose that this occur every day at school."

"We think it is essential to the financial well-being of individuals, families, and our nation that every student is taught how to manage money. We propose that elementary school students and middle school students be taught the fundamentals of money management. We propose that a semester class in personal finance become a requirement for graduation for all high school students."

"Health care costs in the country continue to increase at rates that are far above the overall inflation rate. These costs are increasingly difficult for families, employers, and government. Many illnesses could be prevented or limited through proper wellness laws. We propose that the science curriculum in elementary schools and middle schools include new emphasis on wellness. We also propose that a new course on lifelong wellness become a graduation requirement for all high school students."

"Many students today know very little about the U.S. Constitution, about Veterans Day, about Memorial Day, about the history of the armed forces, and about patriotism. We propose that each school day begin with the Pledge to the Flag followed by reading of two patriotic quotations, which the teacher would then lead a two-minute discussion about."

"Our nation needs more entrepreneurs. Children and teenagers need to know how to start a business. We propose that schools become centers of entrepreneurial knowledge. Ideally, we would like every middle school student to take a class in entrepreneurship followed by a high school class in which students really start a new business. This could be a high school elective class, but we recommend that it be required."

"The nation faces energy problems and environmental problems. School buildings use a lot of energy whether people are there or not, but when the buildings are empty, the energy use does decline. We propose that schools use a four-day work week at the school building with every Friday devoted to providing educational services via the Internet. Think of the savings in energy and in money as the school buses do not run on Friday and the lights are off at school on Friday and the heat and air conditioning systems have little work to do on Friday."

All of those proposals from community groups are well-intentioned. All of those proposals are asking schools to be more than or less than places where the current intended learning is caused. Of course, the curriculum of a school does change from time to time, but the curriculum cannot include every topic that every well-meaning community group advocates.

Even if the intentions of the community groups that made the above six proposals are honorable and valid, schools may not be the best place to implement their recommendations. Schools may have to drop an important part of the current curriculum to add a new topic to the curriculum. When a community group persuades a school board, the state government, or school administrators that the new topic is more important, it may not be possible to simply expand the curriculum. What learning is most important is a filter through which such decisions can be made.

Convincing community groups that schools already have more to do than can fit into the current schedule will not be done without the courage to say "no," but "no" must be said occasionally or often. There is much that community groups can do to support the work of schools; however, seeking to make the schools an extension of a community group's agenda is contrary to the already established purpose of a school.

There are some groups that function as a hybrid for the school and the community. An association of parents, guardians, and educators is one example. An athletic, academic, or fine arts booster group could be another example. These groups can do much good for schools; however, these groups must frequently remind themselves that the purpose of a school is to cause learning and that the school has a document or documents to make it quite clear what learning the school is responsible for. To the extent that these hybrid groups consistently support the school's overall purpose, they provide very valuable services.

We turn now to the media. What can print publications, television, radio, Internet, and other types of media do to support grassroots school improvement? That question and related topics will be explored in the next chapter.

4

Media

Is education the topic that news reporters seek to become experts on as one way to advance their careers, contribute to their profession, and provide highly desired information to readers or viewers? Do other topics—politics, sports, entertainment, economics, traffic problems, severe weather, crime—have more appeal to career-conscious journalists whose employers state that polls of readers and viewers indicate a stronger interest in topics other than education?

There are times when journalists seek to impact public awareness and public opinion. Newspapers could publish a six-part series on how local and state tax systems compare and contrast with tax systems in other localities and other states. Consumer research may not have put tax systems at the top of the list of subjects readers and viewers were asking the media to provide more information about; however, some journalists may have decided that the tax issue needed more attention. One goal could be to increase public demands for tax reform or to stimulate action by political officials, who could work on tax reform initiatives.

Education may not be what readers and viewers tell media consumer research inquiries would be their top choice for more news coverage. If people said they were most interested in weather, sports, and entertainment, would the media omit coverage of other topics? No, but newspapers, newsmagazines, radio stations, television stations, and other media outlets are usually for-profit businesses, so they must pay attention to the preferences of consumers. It is also import for the media to serve the community so an informed citizenry can maintain a vibrant democracy.

Education deserves and needs ample media attention. The media need to include education as one topic that gets substantial attention. Through proper professional coverage of education, the media can cause learning about schools and can contribute to a community's grassroots effort to improve schools.

SCHOOL EFFORTS TO INFORM THE MEDIA

"The people at the schools rarely tell us anything. I assign the reporters from this television station to cover the stories we report on each day. In the old days, groups would mail press releases to tell us about events. We still get information like that, but it is usually sent to us electronically. We know that groups seek publicity, and we do not respond to every notification we get, but some of those electronic press releases are genuinely newsworthy, and we cover those stories that are most important."

"We get sports information from high school athletic directors, or we can check school websites, but even those websites seem to have more information about sports than about anything else at school. I would ask educators to keep us informed. Assign one person at each school to send us information about everything at school. Some of it will turn into stories we can use on our TV news broadcasts."

What can schools do to provide that journalist and other journalists with information that could lead to news stories that make the community more aware of what schools are doing and more aware of what schools need? A list follows, but please add to the list.

1. Send press releases, via traditional mail and electronically, to the media. Include the name of a contact person at the school.
2. Update the school's website daily with news and information that reporters can use verbatim or can use as the start of the reporting they will do.
3. Following all protocols and policies, include photography of school events on the school's website.
4. Create and distribute a press kit about the school so reporters have background information, history, data, statistics, and names of people at the school to contact for details.
5. Have a media day at school to introduce journalists to your school, the people, the programs, the campus, and the current innovations.
6. Invite journalists to be guest speakers for classes.
7. If a student group is in charge of the daily announcements via public address system or television, invite journalists to advise those students about their broadcasts.

8. Survey teachers often to know what upcoming events in classrooms could provide an interesting news story.
9. If the school has a student-written and student-produced school newspaper, send a copy of that publication to local journalists. If there is an electronic version of the school newspaper, send that to local journalists also.
10. Build networks. Some students, faculty, or staff may be related to or friends with local journalists. Use that network to keep local journalists informed.
11.

12.

13.

14.

15.

NEWSPAPERS

Take an inventory, and measure the column inches of stories in the newspaper for the past month to see what topic has had the most coverage. Weekly, daily, local, or regional newspapers can calculate these statistics to see how politics, economics, sports, entertainment, crime, human interest, education, obituaries, weather, and other topics rank in terms of newspaper space allocated to each topic. Are the results what was expected? Are the results what was intended?

Intended? Journalists do not make the news; they report the news. That is true to some extent; however, decisions are made daily in newspaper newsrooms about which stories will be covered and which stories will not be covered. Additional decisions are made about which stories will be on page 1 and how much front page space will be allocated to each of those most prominent stories.

If a high school student can consistently put a basketball through a hoop in a gymnasium, does the newspaper allocate more space to that student than it allocates to the high school student who can more consistently put the right answers on tests? "But how can newspapers publicize every scholar. High school basketball games are public events. Those statistics are made available to reporters. We aren't told about grades. How would we know about every scholar?"

Good question, which good reporters know how to answer. Except for confidentiality limitations due to the ages of students, information about schools is available to any reporter who makes the effort.

"But there is no news most days at schools. Traffic problems, crimes, political scandals, major construction projects, serious fires—these events are serious, are news, and people have told us they want us to provide stories and pictures about these topics. We really don't get many requests to increase the reporting we do about schools."

Schools can make more requests. It may take some effort and some courage. Some educators may think that no publicity is ideal because then people leave the school alone, yet a school that is doing good work or great work has many stories that should be told to the community.

A school that needs various kinds of help could appeal to the community through a newspaper article. Schools and newspapers can be symbiotic. The experiences of one very conscientious reporter and of one very energetic high school principal provide a compelling example.

"I know it is an unusual request, but I think it could be really exciting and important. It certainly makes us stand out from any media competition. Television and radio in our market have never tried anything like this. It could be something readers look forward to and that people talk about. It could make our newspapers stand out. Do I have your approval?" asked the eager reporter.

After a long conversation, the answer was "yes." The reporter's idea was that he become a substitute teacher in the local school district. He had confirmed that more substitute teachers were needed, so his service would be in demand. He could apply to be a substitute teacher today, and if there were no problems, he could be approved in several weeks.

He had talked to a few principals about the idea. Most were intrigued. One high school principal was especially interested but made it very clear that confidentiality limitations had to be followed. Unless students and their parents gave written permission, student names could not be used in any published article.

The work of a substitute teacher had to be done. The journalistic work would be done outside of the school day. The high school averaged seven substitute teachers daily, so he could be assigned to that school each day for a month.

The original plan was to write two articles weekly. That plan was changed because there was so much to write about. Several articles dealt with how physically exhausted the reporter, David Laredo, was at the end of each school day. One article had the headline "Teaching Is Exhausting and Fascinating."

Laredo had a variety of classes to teach, including ninth-grade social studies, tenth-grade world history, Spanish I, Algebra II, computer applications, twelfth-grade English, and physical education during the first two weeks. In four of those classes, he substituted for the same teacher for two consecutive days.

One teacher had to be absent for weeks three and four of Laredo's month at the school. Laredo eagerly accepted that assignment so he could have some continuity with the students and with the subject—junior and sophomore English classes.

Laredo spent extra time talking to teachers on the record and off the record. He spent much time one day each week meeting with the principal. Laredo also talked with school counselors, the assistant principals, the school social worker, the school nurse, the maintenance staff, the cafeteria staff, the librarians, the technology manager, the security officers, and the office staff, including the bookkeeper, the attendance clerk, and the secretaries. He talked to bus drivers. He spoke with parents and guardians. He also thought a lot. His final newspaper article in this month-long series included those lessons learned, emotions felt, and memories created.

"What This Reporter Learned at School"

Teaching is harder than I ever imagined. Teaching is more exhausting than I thought possible. Teaching is fascinating and frustrating, important and underappreciated. Teaching for one month has revealed to me that much great work is being done at North Highland High School. This month of teaching has also revealed to me that the typical approach to solving problems in education does not solve problems but instead creates more problems.

Time. I always thought that teachers had more time than work. The high school schedule at North Highland has each teacher responsible for three ninety-minute block classes that meet every other day. Each teacher has one ninety-minute block daily for planning, grading, copying, computer work. That was never enough time. With six classes to teach, three on what they call "A day" and three more on "B day," a teacher has six classes.

If each class has 25 students, the total per teacher is 150 students. In English classes when my students were given a writing assignment, that meant I had 150 papers to grade. Five minutes per paper means 750 minutes or 12-1/2 hours of grading. Longer papers meant 15 hours or 20 hours of grading. How many jobs create that much extra work for the employee?

The official school day for students is 8:00 a.m. through 3:00 p.m. I would arrive by 7:30 a.m. at first and then 7:15 a.m. when I had the same classes for a two-week period. I stayed at school during those two weeks until 4:00 or 4:30 p.m. and always had two to three hours of work to do at home to prepare lessons and to grade papers.

Count those hours. 7:30 a.m. until 4:30 p.m. plus two to three hours after that. So 11-1/2 hours per day times five means 57-1/2 hours, but that is not all. I did about 10–15 hours of work each weekend during the weeks I had the same schedule of classes. More lessons to plan, even though the regular teacher left lesson plans. I had to prepare and read. Then there were those endless papers to grade. So, add 12-1/2 weekend hours, and the total is 70 hours per week.

It's not just the hours, it's the pace. Teaching is nonstop whenever a teacher has a classroom full of students. You prepare a great lesson, but three students are absent, two students get called to the office, one student falls asleep and blames his part-time job for his fatigue and for him having no homework to turn in, and one student arrives to class late because the guidance counselor had to meet with her.

Then there is a public address system announcement about students who need to leave now for a field trip. Three of my students are on the list for that trip so they leave class. Why was another teacher's field trip more important than the activities I planned for my students? How do I help the students who missed some of class or all of class make up the work? That will take more teacher time, but it is part of the job.

I talked to many teachers during my month of substitute teaching. I also talked to school administrators, school counselors, and staff members. The major concerns were mentioned quite often.

First, educators are asked, make that told, to do much more than educate students. Everything from feeding students breakfast and lunch to stopping bullying between students, from reducing use of tobacco, to reducing teen pregnancy, from stopping students from dropping out of school to convincing students to avoid drugs, from getting students to be physically fit to making students aware of Internet safety issues, from addressing the tragic reality of increased teen suicide to scheduling the many days each year of tests required by the school district, the state government, or the national government.

Teachers and other people at schools realize the importance, possibly life or death in some cases, of these additional responsibilities assigned to schools. Their concern is that as more duties, which are beyond the fundamentals of teaching the required curriculum, get added to what school must do, there is less time for and less concentration on academic instruction in classes. Educators I talked to asked that they be included in any process of making laws, regulations, or policies that mandate what schools must do.

Second, educators said they are concerned that people who never work at a school make decisions that tell people who do work at schools how to do their jobs and what their jobs are. Educators mentioned presidents, Congress, governors, state legislators, school board members, and school district administrators who were never fully informed. What information was usually missing? Input from people who work at schools.

It was interesting that during the month I was a substitute teacher, the state government sent a ten-question online survey to teachers. Few teachers I talked to were impressed with or optimistic about the survey.

As one teacher explains, "I do not do my job online. I teach face-to-face with groups of twenty-five or more students. I get to know each of my students. If the state government people want real input, they need to get out of their offices, away from their computers and meetings. They need to come to our schools and our classrooms to talk with us face-to-face."

I will miss being a substitute teacher. I will miss those seventy-hour weeks, but my employer will find good ways to fill those hours for me. I will miss the students and what we learned together. I will miss the energy of a high school. I will miss the opportunity to touch lives. I will always think of educators, teaching, and schools differently. I hope that my readers are as enlightened about schools as this experience has enlightened me.

The response from newspaper readers was far beyond any expectation of the newspaper editor or of the reporter, David Laredo. Almost all of the calls to the newspaper, e-mails to Laredo, and letters to the editor were positive. This series of articles had informed readers, intrigued readers, inspired readers, and energized readers. A few readers decided to become substitute teachers.

One college student wrote to Laredo to say that she was considering changing her college major so she could become a high school English teacher. A few skeptics wrote letters to the editor stating that Laredo's articles were too supportive of educators, but most letters expressed strong support for teachers and offered ideas for ways the community could help schools.

Laredo's series of articles won several journalistic awards. The newspaper compiled the series into a special section that contained all of the articles and included that special section in a Sunday newspaper edition. Newsstand sales of that Sunday paper were 6 percent above the usual Sunday edition.

Good reporting produced good articles, which evoked much favorable response from readers and which had a positive financial impact on newspaper sales. Much learning about schools was caused. Many offers of support to help schools cause more learning were made. Everyone won.

Some communities have neighborhood newspapers that are published weekly or monthly. Some towns have specialty newspapers, also published weekly or monthly, emphasizing topics of local interest, such as business, entertainment, or sports. Some of these publications could include feature articles about schools, about teachers, about volunteer opportunities at schools, about parent-teacher organizations, about student achievement, or about issues in education that citizens need to know about and become involved in.

As newspapers continue to seek the best balance of the traditional printed paper issue and the innovative electronic version of a newspaper, lessons learned from that transition could be shared with schools. As schools consider electronic alternatives to the traditional textbooks, news organizations could offer perspective and advice. There are many ways that newspapers and schools can work to be mutually beneficial.

TELEVISION

The television camera must have something to show the viewer. The cynic would conclude that the camera's need for powerful signals is why local television news can seem to concentrate on traffic accidents, crimes, and fires. The realist would identify compelling visual opportunities at school for the television news camera to film. This does not mean that schools need to create atypical activities just to satisfy the visual need of television news; rather, this suggests that educators could inform television news professionals of the visual events that naturally occur at school.

It is important to note that some families prefer for their children to not be photographed, interviewed, recorded, or in any way included in school-contained media, such as a school yearbook, or in public-accessed media, such as newspapers, television, or radio. These preferences must be honored, and applicable school district policies must be followed.

The high school marching band is invited to a major celebration or parade in the community. That event will be visual, but so are the rehearsals for the marching band. The media could be invited to after-school rehearsals and to band class. This could help them get background information for a story they do on the day of the parade. This could also be a separate, additional story.

A middle school student sees herself as a future Broadway star. In fact, in her speech and drama elective class, she asked if her class project could be to write, appear in, and direct a short play. The teacher was thrilled with this idea and eagerly guided the talented and ambitious thirteen-year-old.

When the play is presented at a school assembly, which was designed to teach the entire student body how to politely behave at theater and music events plus how to appreciate the work and talent of other students, television cameras would have plenty to see, to film, to capture for a story.

An elementary school's playground equipment was damaged in a storm and needs to be replaced. The faculty of the school decides to make this a learning experience for the students. A television weather reporter comes to the school to explain to the students how strong storms form, why some storms damage property and other storms do no damage, and to answer questions about the weather.

The teachers are impressed with how determined the students are to somehow get new equipment for the playground. Classes do research on the safest, most environmentally compatible, and age-appropriate school playground equipment. The physical education and health teacher works with students on how this new equipment could include physical fitness stations. The math classes research the cost of new equipment. Other classes create ideas for fundraising.

The students create a very formal presentation of their research and of their findings. They have charts, graphs, pictures, and recorded interviews. Television news reporters could find many parts of this playground equipment saga to report on.

Think of the learning that can be caused as the elementary school students apply and develop academic skills to solve the real-life playground equipment problem. The television news reports can enable the community to learn about the work the students are doing. That publicity increases the possibility of community support for the goal the students have set to replace the damaged playground equipment.

No new taxes, laws, regulations, or policies were needed. This is an example of a grassroots effort by many people at the grassroots level to improve a school. There is nothing top-down, bureaucratic, political, or systemic involved.

Television and radio stations have an obligation to provide public-affairs programming or related content. Coverage of school events and issues can help those stations meet those obligations.

Depending upon what else occurs in the community on any given day, high school sporting events can attract none, some, or much media attention. Sporting events will always give the television camera something visual. Media attention is sometimes given to high school athletes when they announce what college they will attend. These events and these announcements are interesting and can merit media attention; however, other events and other announcements at school equally or more certainly merit media attention.

A ninth-grader struggled in all classes but somehow passed each. At the end of ninth grade, a mentoring program at her high school put her in close contact with an advisory team that included a school counselor, a teacher, and a very successful and well-trained high school eleventh-grader. The ninth-grader now had three advocates to whom she was accountable. Her school work improved in tenth grade. Her behavior improved. Her attitude improved. She became active in several school clubs. She became a mentor to a struggling ninth-grader. As a senior, she earned several college scholarships.

Her story merits media attention as much as or more than the story of an athlete and where he will play a sport in college. Journalists can seek such stories. Schools can actively tell journalists about such stories if the student involved and her family agree.

A television station's sales department could work with an advertiser to sponsor the scholar of the week. "Robinson's Bakery is proud to congratulate Samantha Mercer, a senior at North Highland High School. Samantha has a 3.9 grade point average, is senior class vice-president, does volunteer work at her church, and plans to study chemistry in college. Her goals are to be a wife, mother, and pediatrician. Congratulations to Samantha Mercer, this week's outstanding scholar. Samantha's favorite at Robinson's Bakery is our nine-grain bread. Stop by this week for a free slice!"

Some cable television companies are very generous with local-access programming. Some school districts arrange to have their own channels on cable television systems in local markets. Both of these options can be very useful to schools and to school districts.

Students are increasingly technology skilled and video skilled. A television station could host a video contest through which students enter their video on this year's theme, such as "Graduate from high school, do not drop out." The best videos could be broadcast on local television. For the students and for the community, this would cause learning.

RADIO

Radio endures. Despite competition from television for decades and new communication devices in recent years, radio still attracts an audience.

Is there any possible partnership now between radio stations and schools? Some radio stations fill the broadcast schedule each day with syndicated programs that are heard regionally or nationally. There may be little local news on some radio stations. There may be very few locally produced programs on some radio stations.

Some local high school athletic events are broadcast on local radio stations. At halftime of a high school football or basketball game, a profile of each participating school could be provided. Perhaps the principal, a teacher, and a student from each school could be interviewed as part of that profile.

Some radio stations do have local hosts for talk shows and local hosts for music shows, schools could make their administrators, counselors, and teachers available to be on these talk shows. Music teachers and superior music students could be guest hosts on local radio stations that play music.

For radio stations that broadcast local news, school officials can keep the right people at these stations updated on school news just as they keep television station reporters updated.

Radio stations may be willing to help schools promote activities, projects, or issues. Public service announcements that students create about avoiding drugs, including alcohol, and about avoiding tobacco could be broadcast on the radio. Public service announcements about graduating from high school could feature students.

When it is back-to-school time in August, radio stations could have extended interviews with a school district superintendent, with principals, and with teachers to inform the community about how families can prepare for a successful school year.

Radio stations often have items with the station logo. Hats, shirts, key holders, pens, pencils, and similar items could be given to schools for them to use as rewards for students who meet established criteria. A radio station could partner with a school to be the official sponsor of the school's academic honor roll. Every student making the honor roll would be given a radio station logo hat or shirt. Part of what is learned by such actions is that the community notices schools, cares about schools, supports schools, and would like to acknowledge students who are doing what they should be doing—learning.

No Radio Station Is an Island

"There's nothing new in radio. It's music or talk, talk or music. How can our station be unique? We just blend in. We make money, but we could do better. Any ideas?"

The station manager was hoping that someone in the staff meeting would speak up. He did not expect a college student majoring in broadcast communications and doing a summer internship at the station to have the best idea.

The college student said, "My family has lived in this city for generations. My parents and my grandparents always listened to this radio station. Well, they used to. They told me that the station used to have lots of local hosts with local shows. When that changed, they stopped listening to this station except for college sports. And my friends use the Internet or smart phones or other gadgets. I do not know anyone my age who has a radio except in their car. So my idea is to reintroduce radio to the generation of teenagers and young adults who have moved away from radio. I have a plan for how that can be done, but everyone here should add their ideas."

After a long discussion, the radio station manager and the staff plus the intern had created a radio reintroduction plan. Every Thursday evening from 7 p.m. to 11 p.m., the station would target listeners age thirteen to nineteen. That age group would vote via Internet for the songs to be played. Some correspondents from each middle school and high school in the broadcast area would phone in school news on Thursday afternoon and those taped reports, edited if necessary, would be part of the Thursday evening broadcast. Each Thursday evening, two high school students would be at the station to help with and be part of the broadcast.

The radio station got very positive advertiser, listener, and community response to the Thursday evening program. Similar local programs were created for college students, businesses, and entertainment, all with local emphasis and local input. The station learned about the community, the community learned about itself, and the middle school students and the high school students informed the community about schools and often interviewed a teacher or a principal as a guest. Radio was a vibrant part of the community, not isolated as an island.

OTHER MEDIA

The term "media" grows in meaning with each new expansion of the Internet, with each innovative, must-have technology gadget, with more applications of and uses for the Internet, with new features on cell phones, with specialty or niche print publications, with organizations that publish a newsletter in print and/or online, and with every text message or every new website. Schools can team up with some, perhaps many, of these communication methods.

Word of mouth is also within the overall scope of media. When a school takes the communication initiative and keeps students, families, faculty, staff, alumni, taxpayers, and neighbors well informed, there can be a splendid ripple effect of multiplied, beneficial communication.

Finding and Sharing Good Ideas

North Highland High School is one of thirteen schools in the Plymouth County School District. The principals, the superintendent, and some central office workers meet monthly after school late in the afternoon. They meet at a school in a large classroom. The reason for the meeting is not merely to distribute copies of written material that could more easily be sent electronically or to make announcements that could more efficiently be sent electronically.

The reason for these monthly meetings is to have face-to-face, in-person interaction with an emphasis on sharing good ideas. The hope is that each school can learn from every other school. There is no need to pay the high costs of attending conferences out of town when there are many good ideas in Plymouth County that could be shared and implemented.

During the question-and-answer section of one monthly meeting, this question was directed to Beth Ellison, principal of North Highland High School: "What do you do to get so much great publicity about your school? Newspaper, television, radio, everywhere I look or listen, your school is there. What's your secret? Do you have an advertising agency or a public relations firm helping you?"

Beth laughed at the thought that her school could afford or would spend money on advertising or public relations services. She knew that there were ways to get that work done without spending money but with investing time and effort.

Beth responded, "Great question. No, there is not an advertising agency or a public relations firm involved. It's all done through a constant communication process. We keep in touch with the media. We inform the media about school events. We get to know the reporters and build a level of trust, of partnership. We don't ask for or expect favors. Reporters have a job to do, and educators have a job to do. We look for ways to do parts of our jobs together so everyone benefits."

Beth paused for a moment. "OK, I can see that you would like details. Here's the essence of what we do. Every Monday, I send an electronic press release to the media list I have compiled. The press release includes the schedule of events at the school coming up that week, such as special events in classes, guest speakers coming to classes, concerts, theatrical presentations, athletic events, meetings. For extraordinary events, I send out a detailed press release about that one event, such as a band and orchestra concert that includes music professors from the local university who perform with our students at the concert. We constantly tell the stories about the good work that is being done at our school."

Another principal asked a question, "Could you include all of us on the e-mail list of your press releases? I really would like to see how this is done."

Beth was glad to do that. "Sure, I'll send everyone the most recent press release tomorrow, and I'll send the press releases to everyone for the rest of the school year."

Beth Ellison shared a good idea with her colleagues; some of whom will put that idea to use. The results will be good. The community will learn more about the schools. The community will learn about ways to support schools. The grassroots process of trading good ideas and of increasing communications with the community via effective work with the media benefits everyone involved.

This grassroots school improvement is done without new taxes, new laws, new policies, new regulations and without top-down, political, bureaucratic, systemic reform. With that thought in mind, the next topic is elected officials, candidates for public office, and politicians.

5

Elected Officials, Candidates for Public Office, Politicians

Moderator: We welcome our television audience to the third of four debates between the two major political party candidates for governor of our state. John Jackson is currently lieutenant governor of our state. Andrew Adams is a member of the state senate. Both candidates have agreed that our emphasis tonight will be on education. Here is our first question: apparently, there is never enough money for state government—what will you do to be sure that schools in the state are funded adequately?

Mr. Jackson: How we allocate our funds reveals what our priorities are. I will make sure that our top priority is education, and our budget will prove that. In my years as a member of the state House of Representatives, I served on the Education Committee and on the Budget Committee. I know how the process works.

As lieutenant governor, I served on the Education Reform Task Force. The recommendations of that task force would impact all aspects of education. I regret that the state legislature did not approve the bill that would have implemented the education reform plan that the task force created. As governor, I will appoint a new task force to revise those earlier reform plans so our state can lead the nation in education reform and in financial support for schools.

Mr. Adams: I voted against the bill that Mr. Jackson mentioned. There were many reasons to oppose that bill and the ideas it included from the education reform task force. The bill just did not do enough. For years and years, this state has been talking about reforming education. We have taken some action but never enough action. The task force recommendations just did not go far enough. I would reform the education system in this state completely.

I would question everything. Does it make sense to have as many school districts as we have, or could some of them consolidate? Does it still make sense to have a local school board with part-time members making full-time decisions?

Why do we let students drop out of high school? Is money really the issue, or do we provide sufficient money for schools, and we just are not getting the results that money should provide?

So my campaign says to the voters of this state that we need to completely change our system of schools. Little fixes here and there, little reforms now and then are not enough. We need to turn the school system around completely.

Moderator: The first question was about adequate financial support for schools. In the most recent state budget funding, education was cut 2 percent across the board from kindergarten through college. How can we expect more from schools when the schools are given less?

Mr. Adams: Other parts of the state budget were cut also. In fact, all of state government was cut 3 percent except for education, which was cut 2 percent. I have never seen a government budget that was 100 percent efficient or did not have some areas where money could be saved.

I am convinced that the state government does provide adequate financial support for our schools, kindergarten through high school and higher education. Every educator has a role to play in helping the state manage its money well. Every school district and every school must carefully evaluate every item in their budgets. What is essential? What is optional?

I own a business. For three generations, my family has operated a restaurant. There are times when our costs go up, and we have to find ways to stretch dollars, to cut other costs. What works for every business can work for every school.

Mr. Jackson: I disagree. Schools need more money, but state government is not the only source of money for education. Local tax rates can be increased if the people in a school district make that decision to increase local financial support for education. Colleges raise massive amounts of money from their alumni, from grants, from foundations, and from other donors. What keeps elementary schools, middle schools, and high schools from seeking grant money and foundation money? There are financial limits on what state government can do. There are no limits on what local people can do for their local schools.

Moderator: Where will you get ideas for improving education?

Mr. Jackson: As lieutenant governor and as a member of the education reform task force, I have met with several of the most qualified education consultants in the nation. Our task force paid for two of those consultants to visit our state and offer ideas. I was very impressed with the work they had done for other states, and as governor, I would bring those consultants back to our state for further discussions.

I would also take advantage of the many national organizations that can help. Whether it is an association of governors, of legislators, or of educators, these national groups are up to date about the best ideas in the country. I want our state to use the best ideas in the country.

Mr. Adams: I would not pay national consultants. I would work with the colleges and universities of our state. There are college professors who are working with graduate students who are doing important research as they earn advanced degrees in education. For every question that we can think of in education, right here in our state someone is doing research on that topic. I would put that research to good use rather than pay traveling consultants who know very little about our state and who usually have a generic set of ideas they offer to any client who hires them.

Moderator: This question was sent in by e-mail from a viewer: "Both of you are talking about a task force or a reform plan or budget cuts or who you would listen to. Is there any reason why you have not said that you would listen to the teachers, principals, school board members, superintendents, and parents of this state?"

Mr. Adams: Of course, I would listen to those good people of our state. Democracy works best when everyone participates, everyone is heard. The educators in this state are important to every effort we will make to improve education. I do have a concern that current educators may have such a personal stake in the status quo that they may not seek the best ideas from around the nation.

My goal is to have the best schools in the country, so we need to use the best ideas from throughout the country. But the educators in our state are so important to anything we do that I welcome their input and their participation in our work to improve the schools of this state.

Mr. Jackson: I listen to the voters; some of them are teachers, but most of them are not teachers. The voters I listen to tell me that they are not satisfied with so many states doing a better job with education. There is no national measurement of education that shows our state is the best in anything good about schools. What our educators are doing is not making us the best.

Of course, I will listen to educators, but I will listen to many other people also. No one group will be in total control. My administration will be government of all the people, by all the people, for all the people. That's just how democracy should work.

Moderator: I'm looking for specifics with this question. What exact actions will you take to improve schools?

Mr. Jackson: Reform. Reform. Reform. We just are not getting the results we need to get. I would include many more tests to measure progress or the lack of progress. I would reward successful schools, and I would penalize unsuccessful schools. I would lengthen the school year by five instructional days. I would eliminate costly programs that do not work. I would invest in technology to increase the teaching and learning options. I would make sure that we know what is working in other states so we can borrow their best ideas.

Mr. Adams: The state government spends about half of its budget on education. I sometimes think that, as governor, I should spend half of my time on education.

I am interested in finding ways for people in my administration to spend time in schools, me included. We all have heard of presidents of big companies who leave their offices to go work in the stores or in the factories of the company. They always seem to learn a lot when they get back to the grass roots. I think as governor, I should spend a lot of time out in the state instead of just in my office. I should visit schools. Who knows, maybe I could teach a class one day during a visit to a school.

Moderator: As we agreed before this debate, we will take a short break. During this time, the viewers will get to see three commercials from each candidate, chosen by his campaign. When we return, we will use questions that viewers have phoned in or sent to us by e-mail. Mr. Jackson, Mr. Adams, thank you both for your participation. We will be back soon for the rest of our debate.

The second half of the debate had lively, sincere questions, which were followed by standard, memorized answers. When the debate ended, the moderator hosted a discussion with some people who had watched the debate in the television studio as it was broadcast. Some of these audience members were educators. Their comments follow:

"They could save a lot of time and money by asking teachers and counselors and principals what schools need and what schools don't need."

"What works in Texas works in Texas. That does not mean our state needs to copy the Texas school system. Every state is different. Each school is unique."

"The only idea I heard that made sense was to spend more time in schools. I would be impressed with a governor who actually went to a school and taught a class one day. He might decide that being governor and teaching are equally demanding."

"They were so vague. If I gave my students answers like the ones we heard, the students would have to ask more questions. If these candidates are serious about improving education or solving any other problems, they are going to have to be much more specific."

"They convinced me that they are concerned about education. They did not convince me that they know enough about what really happens in schools to be able to get serious. My guess is that neither of them has spent any time in a school for years. If they had been in schools recently, I think they would have told us."

"I'm sure that being governor is a very demanding job. No matter what decisions you make, you will have enemies and critics. Still, they are seeking the job voluntarily. So they must expect some criticism. My concern is that neither candidate seems to trust teachers. They said over and over that most states do a better job with education than our state does. Well, come to my classroom. I put heart and soul into teaching. My students can keep up with any students anywhere. There's no need for a governor to reform my classroom."

"Maybe we could invite whoever wins the election for governor to come to our school and teach. I don't mean to be a guest speaker for a class or to speak at an assembly for the whole school. Let's invite the next governor to come to our school and teach for a full day and to stay after that for a faculty meeting. Imagine how much he would learn about schools. Imagine what our students would learn. It could be great publicity, good politics, and, I hope, good teaching. Why wait? We could invite the current governor. His term ends in a few months, so he probably has the time."

"I never really thought about how much impact politics has on education. The money that comes from the state government is part of the budget that the legislators pass and the governor signs. Laws about testing and other school mandates come from state government. I should pay more attention to politics."

The moderator concluded this discussion by thanking everyone for their attention and their involvement. He encouraged everyone to watch the next gubernatorial debate in one week. The topics then would be the economy, taxes, and the state budget.

What could be accomplished if the candidates for governor each met with the teachers who watched the debate in the television studio? Could they have a productive discussion and find some common ground? Do they speak and think from such different perspectives and life experiences that they would not be able to find common ground?

Do candidates for governor see themselves as becoming "the education governor," which means implementing the largest, most comprehensive, most historic education reform in state history because political reform of education is what proves you are "the education governor"? Is there a way to be "the education governor" without imposing costly, inefficient, temporary, top-down, political, bureaucratic, systemic education reform, which would be replaced in a few years by the state's next "education governor" who has his or her own education reform plan?

Could a governor be one of many people in a state who lead grassroots efforts to improve schools? It may appear idealistic, but the following case study suggests that it is possible.

THE GOVERNOR MEETS THE GRASS ROOTS

"It is my intention to be the education governor but to achieve that status in an unconventional way. I am not proposing any reform of education today. I am not proposing ideas that could become new laws, new regulations, or some new restructuring of the state government bureaucracy as it relates to education."

"Rather, I am on a search for ideas and for problems. I seek to know what is working in our schools and what is not working. Some great work is being done in our schools, and I need to know the inspiring details of that great work. Some serious problems confront our schools, and I need to know the realistic details of those problems. And where schools are not getting great results, I need to know why."

"There are sixty-two school districts in our state. When the school year begins in August, the lieutenant governor and I will spend one day per week visiting two different school districts. Our time will be mostly in schools so we can talk with people who are on the front lines of education, the people who are working daily at the grass roots."

"By the end of this school year, every school district in our state will have been visited by the lieutenant governor or me. We will take a few staff members from our offices and from the state department of education with us on each visit so we get more thorough input at each school district. We will compile that input as we return from each visit. Then we will combine the lessons learned, ideas suggested, problems identified, suggestions for solutions provided, and other input into our comprehensive state-of-the-schools report. This report will be available in print and online to everyone in our state for their consideration and response. Once we have that final round of input, we will be ready to make recommendations about how to improve schools in our state."

"I should mention there will be time for public comment and input when we visit each school district. We will spend most of our time in schools, in classrooms, in hallways, in the cafeteria to see school life as it really is and to hear about school life as it really is. We will schedule time for parents, guardians, community members to offer input during our visit to each school district."

"We begin our visits in three weeks. We will have our completed, comprehensive report in one year. May this be the beginning of the most successful school improvement effort in our state's history."

It was exactly that—the beginning of the most successful school improvement effort in the state's history. After visiting all of the school districts in the state and many different schools throughout the state, the governor, lieutenant governor, and their staffs completed a thorough report filled with examples of what was working well, with descriptions of new and old problems that schools confront daily, with examples of what was not working well, and with verbatim comments that very honestly described the reality of school life, be it good, bad, or in between.

The governor himself wrote the introduction to the comprehensive report. His introduction follows:

"Thousands and thousands of voices across our state have been heard. Your convictions are deep. Your concerns are genuine. Your optimism is inspiring. Your commitment is exemplary. Your ideas are powerful. The problems you face are numerous, complex, and complicated, yet you honorably persist."

"You have explained and you have shown what is working well in our schools. This report includes many examples of great work being done in classrooms and throughout schools. All schools can benefit from knowing what is working in schools across the state. We encourage educators to borrow these great ideas, making changes and adaptations as needed in your unique school."

"You have also explained what is not working in schools and the problems schools face. We observed some of these situations and conditions. Some of these situations can be corrected with a more serious work ethic, with changes in instructional methods, and with schools getting more serious about academics. Some of these situations will require major commitment by an entire community to solve or improve."

"You have told us that the state government makes the work educators do at schools harder and more complicated than necessary. You spoke of mandates imposed by state government that you had no input on or notice about. You spoke of laws passed by the legislature and signed by the governor that were created with good intentions but that were completely unrealistic and that had little or no input from the educators whom the laws would most directly impact."

"Those of you who have been in education for many years told us to quit reinventing education laws and regulations every few years. You said that those changes consume time, effort, and money but rarely accomplish much. You said that state government acts as if its bureaucracy was more important than your classrooms."

"Please read this report. Please think a lot about what you read. By October 1 of this year, you are encouraged to provide your additional ideas and comments. All of that input will then be considered along with this report as the foundation for school improvement proposals I will make to the legislature next January. I can assure you of this, my proposals will reflect your grassroots insights and ideas. My proposals will be of, by, and for our schools, our people, our state—not of, by, and for the state government and its education bureaucracy."

"You have told us that the top priority of a school is for each student to learn. As that priority guides your work and your decisions, that priority—to maximize learning by each student—will guide the actions taken by state government. As all of us direct our work, our decisions, and our actions to support that highest priority, we will see the school improvement that all of us seek."

We can again thank Dr. Earl Reum for his insightful words of wisdom, "People support what they help create." Elected officials, candidates for public office, politicians who apply Dr. Reum's wisdom are true to the essence of democracy. Citizens who communicate with and monitor the actions of elected officials, candidates for public office, and other politicians are supporting democracy through participation. No person will get everything they seek from the political process. No politician will get a 100 percent approval rating. Democracy's process can get a 100 percent approval rating. When actions to improve education are founded on broad input, the results are much more likely to be successful because the actions taken were practical, realistic, feasible, and ready to be implemented by people who helped create them.

"People support what they help create" suggests that people can easily oppose or resent what is imposed upon them. No one governor has all of the answers. No one person's ideas shared with a governor will be adopted unchanged and without other ideas included.

The process of listening to each other or reasoning together, of finding common ground, and of respectfully and politely disagreeing or creating a great idea out of several good ideas is a process that builds support for and commitment to the decisions that are made and the actions that are taken. Politicians and their constituents can benefit from abiding by the process of working together toward a shared goal—to improve schools—and a shared purpose of schools—to cause learning.

Evaluate this statement: our schools are not perfect; therefore, school reform by government action is necessary. Are new laws, in this case laws mandating certain school reform actions, the solution for problems in education? Are schools imperfect because our laws about education are too few in number and too limited in impact?

To every problem in school is there an equal and opposite solution that comes through the political, bureaucratic, law-making process? No. Laws can be helpful, but the wrong law written with the wrong information mandating the wrong programs for schools to implement is counterproductive.

One sixteen-year-old loves to read. Another sixteen-year-old avoids reading. The first sixteen-year-old is from a family where reading was encouraged, where books were plentiful, where visits to the public library were frequent, and where each family member read each day. This was done because the family made reading a high priority, not because of a social engineering mandate from government.

The second sixteen-year-old is from a family where reading rarely happened. Would a law have changed that? No. When the student was in kindergarten and in the early elementary grades, her school could have intervened to be sure she mastered reading and to be sure she always had a book checked out from the school library to discuss with a librarian after reading it.

No law was needed; rather, a grassroots effort at a school by teachers and the librarian makes a difference. Schools need not wait for new laws to implement what concerned, determined, and energetic educators can do. New laws and new education reforms are unnecessary when effective grassroots efforts lead the way, take the initiative, and get results. Education reform is moot when abundant learning is already happening.

THE CANDIDATE AND THE CONSULTANT

"We are honored that you have chosen our political consulting and campaign management firm to work with your campaign as you seek the nomination for governor. As you know, in recent years, we have worked with many candidates who were involved in primary elections or general elections for the United States House of Representatives, for the United States Senate, for governor, for other state offices, for mayor of some very large cities, and for two people who sought presidential nominations."

"We know what works in political campaigns. From advertising to press releases, from campaign events to positions on the issues, from speech writing to public opinion poll taking and analysis, we are ready to offer every service your campaign needs."

The candidate listened closely and then spoke, "All of that sounds good. Let's avoid one problem. I do not want the press in this state to say that my campaign is a paint-by-number scheme that your company puts together, which is just like every other campaign your company runs. Don't give me a speech on job creation that is the same speech used by a candidate for governor whose campaign you managed last year in another state."

The vice-president of the consulting company knew what to say, as would be expected of campaign experts. "Of course. You are a unique candidate, and this is a unique state. We do want to give you the advantage of campaign methods that have worked in other states, and we want to steer you away from campaign methods that our analysis confirms do not work. I hope that is reasonable."

The candidate was satisfied for the most part. "Let's get started. Nothing generic. Nothing recycled from your recent campaigns. Our citizens are concerned about the economy and about education. Those are two major topics. We'll discuss the economy later when my economic advisors can join us. Let's discuss education and what ideas I should support or oppose."

The consultant was ready. "Candidates we have worked with in recent years have had much campaign success with a clear and targeted concentration on accountability and results. The taxpayers respond well with votes when a candidate convinces them that the tax money put into education will not be an endless flow but will be earned."

"This means that test scores and other quantitative measurements are used to evaluate teachers, principals, schools, and school districts. This means that the old-fashioned calculation of pay is no longer used. In the old system, the more college degrees and the more years of experience you had in education, the higher your pay. Voters like merit pay. If your students do the best work as shown in test scores and other measurements, you get the most pay or you get some salary increment." The consultant paused as the candidate had a question.

"To my knowledge, no school district, and for that matter no state, has created a reliable and fair system of merit pay. Can you imagine the court challenges if we used a merit-pay system based on certain tests that students take? No test is perfect, so no merit-pay structure based in part or in whole on tests could survive a court challenge. If I run on this idea, I am asking for serious problems later." The consultant must have heard that question before because he had a quick answer.

"The goal is to win the election. You hired us to be your campaign consultants and to help manage your campaign. The voters in state after state are not impressed with the same old promises. They have to hear something new, different, and bold. Telling the voters that pay in education will be tied to results in schools speaks the language of today's voter. College professors and education consultants who create innovations for schools have offered merit-pay plans."

"You are right. Those plans are complex and controversial. Few of those plans have been implemented, but the concept of merit pay for educators is one that voters like. It is a campaign approach that separates you from your competitors. This issue can help you win. Winning is why you are running, and winning is why we are involved with your campaign."

The candidate was still uneasy. "Merit pay is a bold concept. No doubt, it could get applause from an audience at a campaign event. It could get some votes for me. But if it cannot be implemented in a fair and practical way, then it is a false promise at worst and a questionable promise at best."

The consultant was ready. "We understand your concerns. We brought four merit-pay plans for you to read. Two of these are from college professors of education, and two of these are from well-known public policy think tanks. You can solve the problem of how to implement merit pay by setting up a task force of educators, legislators, community members, business leaders, and other people."

"It becomes the duty of the task force to write the recommendation for how to implement merit pay. That way you get the campaign benefit of an idea the voters like, merit pay, and you show that you listen to the citizens of this state by involving them in implementing merit pay. You are bold, and you are democratic; you are seeking solutions, and you are listening to voters, to citizens."

The meeting continued, and the merit-pay idea was likely to become part of the candidate's set of promises. The consultant showed examples of compelling television commercials that featured the merit-pay idea. The candidate had to agree that the commercials were strong and could be persuasive.

He did have doubts that merit pay would be implemented due to issues of fairness and due to political realities of getting a merit-pay bill through the state's legislature. Perhaps it was worth a try. It could be a bold campaign gesture. It could certainly stimulate some discussion and reaction. Maybe that was what the candidate's campaign needed, but is that what was best for education?

As it worked out, the candidate did not endorse merit pay but did propose a task force to study the idea and to make a recommendation. The candidate thought this was a more reasonable approach. The consultant thought this was a less bold and less impactful approach. What do you, the reader, think?

LETTERS TO THE CANDIDATE

"I watched the debates last week that you and your opponent had. I paid very close attention. I am a retired teacher, so I was especially interested in what both of you said about education. To be honest, I was not impressed."

"The ideas that you offered just will not work. More testing, are you serious? Do you realize how much time is already taken in schools for testing that is required by the local school board, by the state department of education, and by the national government? Enough is enough."

"More testing is not needed. Teachers measure the achievement of students day to day with grades. Ask any conscientious teacher how any of his or her students is doing, and they can tell you a lot more than any expensive statewide or national test can tell you."

"I would encourage you to think of what the state government could do less of in education. Begin with less testing so teachers have more time for more teaching, please."

"I'm sure it is difficult to be a candidate for governor. People criticize you no matter what you say or do. You have to raise all that money. It is not easy, but you volunteered to run for governor, so I guess you knew what you were getting into."

"Here's my complaint. You have never been a teacher. You have never worked in a school. I can't find any evidence that you have done volunteer work at a school. So how do you suddenly know what schools need? You have all of these big, fancy ideas, but how do you know that any of them can help?"

"I would suggest that people who run for office need to spend more time listening to voters and less time talking at the voters. As for what to do about education or getting new businesses to come to this state or cleaning up the environment, go listen to educators and business operators and scientists. Listen to what those experts think. They work in those areas every day. Listen to them."

"I ran for office myself a few times. I was mayor of my hometown, and then I was in the state House of Representative for eight years. Since then, I have helped some friends when they ran for public office, and I keep in touch with people to be sure my voice is heard."

"I would like to give you some advice. I think you could be a good governor. I am more impressed with you than with your opponent. Here's my advice—when you make your television commercials, just look right into the camera, and tell us what you are going to do. Do not bad-mouth your opponent. Do not use Hollywood special effects. Just tell us your ideas."

"When I was in the state House of Representatives, I served on the Education Committee. It bothered me that most of the testimony we heard came from people who were bureaucrats from the state Department of Education. I always asked those people how long it had been since they worked in a school. The answer was five years, ten years, or longer. Some of them had never worked in a school. How can they give the legislature good information if they just sit in an office?"

"So my advice to you, no matter whether the topic is education or something else, is to keep in touch with people who know the facts. The ideas you support will be only as good as the accuracy of the information you are given."

"I know you want to be a very active governor. You have big plans to change the tax system, to create jobs, to improve roads, and to fix schools. Please, slow down, at least with schools. I was in education for thirty-three years. I have seen governors and their big education reform plans come and go. The big changes never work very well, if at all."

"My idea is that, during the next two years, we pass no new laws about education. Just give the educators the next two years to do their jobs without a ton of new laws and regulations that people at schools have to figure out and adjust to and attend meetings on and fill out reports on. Just let them teach for the next two years. My guess is the results would be so good that we could add two more years of no new laws or regulations."

"Schools are not good because of new laws or regulations. Schools are good because of work done by good teachers, counselors, principals, and staff members. Please remember that."

"I don't expect you to fix everything in our state. I expect the people who live here to do their part. That's why I visit my youngest daughter's high school every year. I spend two or more full days at her school. I visit classes. I am in the cafeteria at lunch. I am in the hallways when students move to their next class."

"I see some great teachers, some ordinary teachers, and a few weak teachers. I don't get it. Right there in the same building are some great teachers, and in the next room, there could be a teacher doing nothing but worksheets and videos. Fixing that is not a job for the governor. Fixing that is a job for all of the people at the school, so I always give the principals a report of what I see at the end of each of my visits."

"More people doing things like that at the grassroots level could do a lot of good, probably more good than some plan you would try to do from the state capital that is supposed to solve every problem in every school all across the state. I'm sure you can help and that state government can help, but local people need to take the lead on their local problems."

With that thought in mind, we will consider voters, citizens, and taxpayers in the next chapter.

6

Voters, Citizens, Taxpayers

Government can do less if citizens will do more. Government can impose fewer top-down, political, bureaucratic, systemic reforms of education filled with new laws and regulations if citizens initiate more grassroots actions to improve schools. Part of the price of schools being liberated from top-down reform is for the people associated with each school to be so productively active in causing learning through grassroots efforts that it is fully obvious that no top-down reform is needed.

Voters, citizens, taxpayers can begin their efforts with a certain awareness that any politician's campaign promise to "fix education" is impossible to keep. The politician is not being dishonest or deceptive with the promise. He or she is a politician, which means that he or she is in the arena where problems in society get addressed with laws.

"If there is something wrong with education, we will fix the laws, and that will fix the schools." If school problems were solved merely by passing new laws, there would be few, if any, school problems because laws about education have been passed for centuries.

Because public school districts within states are paid for with taxpayer funds, of course public laws govern those schools. Governing the public school system in a state through the state constitution and subsequent laws involves establishing, maintaining, and occasionally updating the legal structure of the school system. Those laws will not be the reason a school is great, average, or below average. Those laws will not transform a below average student into a scholar.

But can't laws be written in such specific ways to micromanage and to micro-measure schools? Can't laws and regulations control what happens and what does not happen in every classroom? Despite the abundance of laws about education, have all of the desired results been obtained? No. There is simply a limit to what laws can accomplish in and for education. There is not a limit to what dedicated, honorable, goal-oriented, purpose-driven people at the grassroots level can accomplish in and for education.

A student is having trouble with reading. The teacher spends extra time with that student before school twice a week, and it helps. The teacher arranges for the school counselor, who once worked as an elementary school reading specialist, to work one-to-one with the student twice each week. The student's family is told what can be done at home to encourage reading and to build reading skills.

Two retired teachers, whose careers were at this same school, volunteer one day each week to work with individual students or small groups of students. A group of local citizens creates a book donation program so people can easily donate used, but no longer needed, books from their homes for use at the school through the school library. The total result of these actions is that the original student who struggled with reading is now quite skilled in literacy; plus, many other students are getting the direct, personal guidance they need. The grassroots effort was successful and precluded any real or imagined need for imposed reform.

Voters can, should, must participate in elections. School board elections are opportunities for voters to clearly express their priorities about education. Candidates for school board seats may hold town meetings or neighborhood meetings where local voters can ask questions. Attend those meetings, and ask questions such as those listed below and those you add to this list:

1. What will you do to be sure that all schools are funded adequately?
2. What policies do you think are needed to deal with increasing problems of social-network communications between students during school hours and between a teacher and a student at any time?
3. How often do you intend to visit schools, including observing in classrooms, or do you not see this as part of your job as a school board member?
4. Our schools spend a lot of time on required tests. Do you think we spend a proper amount of time on this, too much time, or too little time?
5. What would you do to increase involvement at schools by parents and guardians?
6. The middle school and high school students who are in sports and other extracurricular activities barely have to earn an overall passing average. As I understand it, they could make a D grade in each class and still participate. I would recommend a required C grade in each class to be eligible. What do you think the requirement should be?

7. I have heard from people that some schools are very serious about discipline, but other schools are pretty weak with discipline. How would you address this?
8. A lot is done in this school district for students who are at risk of failing or who need some special help. Those programs are important. We don't do as much for gifted and talented students, who can be at risk in a different way. They can be at risk of their inherent academic ability never being fully challenged and developed. What would you do to support gifted and talented educational programs?
9. Are all of the jobs that exist at the school district's central office really needed? Budgets are tight, and schools are told to save money or that some program is being eliminated due to costs. What would you do to be sure that every position at the central office is completely essential? Most people I talk to think that some of those jobs could be eliminated without causing the types of problems that happen when a job at a school is eliminated.
10. This district spends a lot of money on bus transportation to get students to school and back home. Are we required to do that? I just think that if parents and guardians had to get their children to schools, the families might get more involved with school. We transport the students, we feed the students, and we provide all kinds of other services in addition to education. Some people really need all of that, but other people just take advantage of the system. A family that gets their child the newest cell phone but claims they can't pay for school lunch is not being honest.
11. Some school districts have their own school security officers. These law enforcement experts work directly in the schools, especially in the high schools. Do you support a program like that for our school district?
12. There is a lot of talk about the achievement gap, but what gets done about it? Do you think the achievement gap is a real problem, or is it just some trendy social engineering issue? If it is a real problem, what do you think needs to be done?
13. What do you think is the most important goal our schools should have? Above all else, what is most important, you know, the real reason schools exist more than anything else?
14. What do you think is the best way to improve schools?
15.

16.

Now, using some of those questions, let's visit a community forum featuring three people who are running for a seat on the local school board. Each candidate will answer the questions. Room will be provided for the reader to also answer the questions. After reading the answers, including those of the reader, decide which candidate would win the election and why.

Moderator: Students may participate in sports or other extracurricular activities if they have a D grade or better in each class they are taking. Do you think this requirement is adequate or not?

Candidate 1: It is my understanding that our schools use the grading standard that the state's high school athletics organization has set. I would support continued compliance with that plan because almost all schools use that requirement. A few schools have set additional requirements, but because some students move from school to school or from school district to school district, it seems simple and fair to have the same rule in as many schools as possible.

Candidate 2: I would raise the standard. To be involved in any activity, a student must have a C grade or better in every class. That is not a C average overall where three A grades make up for three F grades or three B grades make up for three D grades. I would go one step further. If a student is ever suspended from school for discipline reasons, the student is not eligible for any extracurricular activities for one month after returning to school from the suspension.

Candidate 3: This is the type of decision that each school should be allowed to make. The circumstances at each school are unique. What works with extracurricular participation is not the same at each school. This is one of many topics that I would encourage the school board to stay out of. We have school district finances to work on and compliance with state or federal laws to worry about. Many other matters are best left to each school to take action on or to leave as they are.

Reader:

Moderator: What do you think is the best way to improve schools?

Candidate 1: Do not tolerate failure, and do not tolerate misbehavior. This would apply to students and to school district employees. I hear from principals and teachers about defiant middle school or high school students who refuse to do any work, who disrupt classes, who skip classes.

I would suggest some version of three strikes and you are out. Three suspensions from school for discipline reasons and you finish the school year at the alternative school; plus, you stay at the alternative school for the next school year. Maybe you stay there permanently because it might work better for you and it keeps you from disrupting classes at your former school.

I would also evaluate teachers and principals very closely based on student achievement, plus on factors such as employee attendance. The teacher whose absence or absences each month always come on Friday is not sick but is creating three-day weekends at taxpayer expense.

Candidate 2: The best way to improve schools is to fully enforce all the laws we have now about schools and all of the regulations. Do you know that there is a state regulation saying schools will make every effort to have every elementary school student at grade level for reading? Do we know if schools are making every effort on this? School boards can perform an oversight function to be sure that laws and regulations and policies are completely enforced.

Candidate 3: I doubt that there is one best way to improve all schools. It's like saying there is one best medicine to give all people who are sick or one best treatment to give all people who are injured. The people and the situations at each school are different.

I do think we need to reconsider the idea that every student must go to college. There are many good technical and vocational careers that do not require college. What's wrong with letting middle school and high school students begin training for technical and vocational careers? Be sure they master the academic basics, but create training and skill-building and credentialing programs that lead to good jobs and that some students would commit to much more than years of typical classroom work.

Reader:

Moderator: Some school districts have their own school security offices. Do you support a program like that for our school district?

Candidate 1: I have read a lot about these resource officer programs or school law enforcement programs. I would prefer to install security cameras throughout our school buildings and the school campuses. The cameras could record any incidents and provide proof of who did what. The school administrator could use that evidence to resolve the situations. The one-time cost of buying and installing cameras is probably less than the recurring cost of more employees; plus, the cameras can be everywhere, and no school administrator or law enforcement officer can be everywhere.

Candidate 2: I support this. I would put at least two school law enforcement officers in each high school. I would have one or two law enforcement officers assigned to the middle schools on a rotating basis. I would have an officer assigned to elementary schools to go into classrooms and work with the teachers on the curriculum aspects of good school citizenship and good community citizenship, plus to help with any situations that can occur even with the youngest students.

Our employees, our students, and our visitors deserve to have their safety protected. Also, these school buildings are very costly investments. I would seriously consider having an additional officer who patrols our campuses at night throughout the year, summer included. Vandalism and other crimes that we prevent would be ample justification for this investment in that additional officer.

Candidate 3: I really don't like the appearance of uniformed officers on patrol in our schools. Has it really come to this? Maybe I am out of touch with modern times, but I hate to think that we need police officers in our school hallways. It wasn't like that when I was in school.

Reader:

Based on those answers, does one candidate impress you more than the other two candidates? Were your answers to the questions better than the answers given by these candidates? Are you in a job and life position where you could run for the local school board? If not, perhaps you could encourage a friend to run and then help with the campaign.

At the individual school level, there will sometimes exist a school council. This group might be called the "site-based council" or the "school improvement council/committee." Membership will vary but could include a principal, some teachers, some parents or guardians, a classified employee, a community member, and a student. Student membership may be nonvoting and may be more likely at high schools if it is included at all.

Consider a middle school that is part of a school district that, by school board decision several years ago, requires each school to have a school improvement council. The principal is automatically a member of this council. The faculty members elect two teachers to be on the council. Parents and guardians elect two additional council members. The classified staff at the school elects one member to be on the council. Council meetings are open to everyone at the school and to the public. The council serves as an advisory board to the principal on curriculum, instruction, scheduling, testing, budgeting, extracurricular programs, and use of the school building.

The four parent-guardian candidates for the council are guests at a meeting of the school's parent association. Each of the candidates presents an opening statement, and then questions are taken from the audience. The number of people who vote in the parent-guardian election is usually very small contrasted with the large number of parents or guardians whose children attend the middle school. A few people who do show up to vote on election day can determine the outcome.

The opening statements of the four parent-guardian candidates are below as are two questions and their answers. Consider what they have to say, and then reflect on what you, the reader, would think of these candidates. Which two would you vote for? If you were the fifth candidate, what would your opening statement include, and how would you answer the questions?

OPENING STATEMENTS

Candidate 1: I really believe in the concept of a school improvement council. People at each school can take actions. No need to wait for the state government. No need to wait for the school district. We can take action. My biggest concern is curriculum. The middle school curriculum is the same stuff every year. The students take math, science, social studies, and English. They've been taking all that since they began elementary school. The curriculum is old and ordinary. I would like to see us update and innovate.

Candidate 2: The school improvement council is a very good idea, but it has not been implemented well. As this meeting tonight shows, either very few people know about the council or very few people care enough to attend a meeting like this. We have four candidates, and about twenty people in the audience. There are seven hundred students in the school. There must be well over one thousand parents of those students, plus the guardians. We have twenty out of one thousand here tonight. My goal is to increase involvement of parents and guardians in this council and in school overall. If we increase that involvement, we'll have the manpower to accomplish anything.

Candidate 3: I think we have a good school. My oldest son went here and did great in high school and is doing great in college. My middle son and my youngest son are here now. They make good grades. They stay out of trouble. I wish they had to work harder. I mean, they don't do much homework, but they make A and B grades all the time. They tell me they do everything they can to get extra credit points that seem to help keep their grades up. But they need to be challenged more.

So I'm most interested in working on the curriculum and on how students are taught. My oldest son tells me that his senior-year English class was harder than most of his college classes have been. He said it was because they had so much challenging reading to do and to write about. I think our students need more of that in middle school.

Candidate 4: I really want to see many more parents and guardians get involved at school. There is no reason for people who volunteered when their children were in elementary school to stop being involved when their children are in middle school or even in high school.

There are so many ways that volunteers can help at school. I think it is important for parents and guardians to visit classes their children take. So that's a summary of my reasons to run for this. Well, one more reason: I have some real concerns about using technology too much in school. I know that students need technology skills. Their jobs in the future, no matter what they do, will use computers and the Internet.

I just want to be sure they can read and write and think on their own, without machines. If you can read, write, and think and then express yourself well in speaking, you can do almost anything. I just don't want our students to be technology skilled, but reading, writing, and arithmetic unskilled. Let's not abandon the time-honored basics.

Reader:

Moderator: Our school prides itself on a very successful band, orchestra, and choral music program, but we know that test scores show little progress in math and English during the past few years. What can be done to get math and English up to the level of our music classes?

Candidate 1: Let's find out what is working so well in music classes and see if some of that could work in other classes. Students usually like music. I mean, they listen to popular music a lot. You can't say that they spend the same free time on math and English like they do on music. Plus, many of the music students chose to take their music class. All of the students have to take math and English, so the comparison is not exact. Still, I would see what teaching methods are working in music and try to apply those methods to other classes.

Candidate 2: I really think volunteers can help. The students who struggle with math or English could benefit from having a mentor who tutors them individually. If we recruit parents, guardians, community members, and former teachers to come help work with those students, it could do a lot of good, and it costs no money. The taxpayers should like that.

Candidate 3: It would not surprise me if some of the seventh and eighth graders just get tired of the same old math every year. Let's teach algebra in seventh grade and geometry in eighth grade after a thorough and demanding sixth-grade-year of the fundamentals of math and some pre-algebra.

I have been on this school's curriculum committee. We have spent a lot of time this year on math. I would enact the committee recommendation, which is seventh-grade algebra and eighth-grade geometry. Challenge the students. They will rise to the occasion. Low test scores could mean low challenge as much as it means low understanding.

Candidate 4: I have visited a few math classes here. They use calculators all the time. They know how to punch buttons and enter numbers. They cannot explain what the numbers are doing or what the numbers mean. They just punch buttons and write down the answer on the screen. Teach them how to think so they can explain if an answer makes sense. With English, one part of the problem is they expect the computer to do the spelling for them. They also expect the Internet to do the writing and the research for them. Every now and then, make them take a pencil and a paper so they do math problems by hand and so they write paragraphs by hand.

Reader:

Moderator: Money is always a concern for schools. What ideas do you have to help our school improvement council budget our school-based funds well?

Candidate 1: Council members have a training program to attend, and part of what we are taught deals with school-level budgeting policies and procedures, plus how to avoid mistakes. I do the accounting and billing for the business our family owns. With the training I would get and the experience I bring, budgeting would be a strength I bring to the council.

My hope would be that we allocate funds according to our priorities and that means academics. Unless certain money must go to specific expenses other than academics, I would direct funds to support teaching and learning above all other matters. As a taxpayer, I would expect school funds to support academics, teaching, and learning above all else. Isn't that what school is for?

Candidate 2: My emphasis is to increase parent and guardian involvement. I would be interested in two ideas that relate to budgets. Let's e-mail to every family we have e-mail addresses for a copy of the council's approved budget. We'll send another copy home with each student as a backup. Let's ask for ideas and feedback in the budget. That might be the first time some parents or guardians felt that their opinion was sought, and that could lead to some new involvement. We may have funds, or we may need to raise funds, but some parents or guardians may not have transportation to school, so that keeps them from volunteering or visiting.

Through our budget or our fundraising, let's get bus vouchers or taxi vouchers for these families. We could also set up a buddy system for carpooling. People in each neighborhood of our attendance area could help transport each other to and from school for meetings, visits, and volunteer work.

Candidate 3: My priority is to academically challenge all of the students, so I would like to see our budget allocations for instructional materials and for library books include more advanced content. I've been in our library, and it is so well run. The students like to go there, but most of the books are for middle school readers or actually for lower grade levels. We need to address all reading levels, so let's not overlook the students who read far above middle school level.

Candidate 4: You know my concern about excessive reliance on technology. The right amount of technology use at school is good. Too little technology or too much technology, both of those are problems. I will watch the budget closely to see that, when we spend money on technology, it is the right amount and it is for the right reasons.

Reader:

Notice the interests and concerns of these four candidates for the school improvement council as reflected in these answers—curriculum, parent and guardian involvement, challenging students, the right uses of technology. These grassroots topics can directly and favorably impact education at school where it matters most—in the classroom. These answers also show the importance of building family and home involvement in education.

The classroom and the home are the grass roots at the most fundamental levels. This school improvement council could apply the answers of these four candidates to create true school improvement by enhancing the learning experience of each student, of all students. That is an example of what grassroots school improvement can do directly, efficiently, and personally. Top-down political, bureaucratic, systemic reforms are not known for being direct, efficient, or personal.

The people who will respond to the candidates for a seat on the school board or a position on a school improvement council are voters, citizens, and taxpayers, all three. Some of these people are parents; some of these people are guardians; however, in school board elections, some or many of the voters may not have family members who attend public schools. The community in which they live and where they are a voter, a citizen, a taxpayer needs their informed involvement in school improvement efforts.

At the beginning of or at the conclusion of school board meetings, time is occasionally or regularly included for public comment. How could a taxpayer participate in this setting? Consider the following input from two taxpayers at the conclusion of a local school board meeting:

Taxpayer 1: This has been a very interesting meeting. There were reports about many different topics. There were some decisions made and some decisions postponed. I know your work is demanding. As a taxpayer, I would like to ask a question. How do you know that your current budget is the best for students? Is everything in the budget allocated with student achievement as the guiding priority, or is some of the money spent just because it has always been spent that way whether it has been evaluated as helping student achievement or not? What I'm getting at is, for lack of any better term, student achievement-based budgeting.

You know the concept of zero-based budgeting where every part of the budget has to be justified anew each year or it is reduced to what can be justified or some parts could be eliminated. If what we are about is student achievement, then evaluate every dollar in the budget according to how effectively that dollar increases, enhances, supports student achievement. If you set up a taxpayer group to help analyze the budget this way, I would be glad to serve on that group.

Taxpayer 2: I also speak to you today as a taxpayer. I am told that some schools have no money to buy new textbooks. I am told that in some classes, there are not enough textbooks for every student to have one to use all year at home and at school. The limited copies of the textbook have to stay in the classroom so all students can use them during their class. It wasn't that way when I was in school. It should not be that way now.

I notice that money was recently spent to upgrade athletic facilities at several schools. What was wrong with the old facilities? Were they unsafe, or were they just not as fancy as what other school districts have? Until every student has a textbook for every class, I would suggest that we find other areas of the budget to cut, whether it is athletic facilities, expensive field trips, or expensive trips that district employees take to attend educational conferences.

It probably costs $2,000 for one person to attend that conference I saw was approved tonight, the conference in California in January. Wouldn't using that money to buy thirty or forty textbooks get a better return on investment than one person going to a conference? That person can read a book or two written by the conference guest speakers and save $1,950, assuming the two books read cost $25 each.

Please look for ways to provide textbooks for all students in all of their classes before we put up a new scoreboard at the ball park or before we send anyone to another conference. Our priority is for students to learn, not for scoreboards to have fancy graphics or employees to take fancy trips.

These two taxpayers brought vital perspectives to the school board meeting. It took some time and effort to attend the meeting, but for grassroots efforts to work and for grassroots efforts to prevent top-down mandates, time and effort from voters, citizens, and taxpayers are essential.

Consider now the comments of one additional citizen who attended a school board meeting and who spoke to the board at the conclusion of the meeting.

"I wish I could be a taxpayer. I used to be a taxpayer. I used to own a home. I used to pay property taxes. My wife and I both worked hard. We had big hopes for our children. My son and my daughter are in middle school. They are good students. We make sure they do their homework. We make sure they get to the bus stop on time every day. In the past six months, my wife and I both lost our jobs. We also lost our house because I could not make the payments. We moved in with my parents, but it is really crowded there, and they can't pay their bills and our bills!"

"So I want you to know that the school district is essential to our family. You feed my children breakfast and lunch every day at no charge to me. Thank you. They need to eat, and it would be hard for me to pay for those bills. You provide bus transportation for my children. Thank you. I had to sell my car two months ago. I need your help to get my children to school and back home."

"That weekend partnership you created with a local food bank, a bakery, a local clothing bank, the public library, and some churches is such a blessing to our family. I think the social worker at the middle schools in this district set it up. On Fridays, at the time right after school and before the buses leave, students who need it and if their families qualify, get weekend food. It gets my children through Saturday and Sunday. Sometimes, the package includes a book, toothpaste, and soap. Once a month, the package includes a shirt and a pair of pants. My children never go hungry because this school district and donations from this community are giving them the extra help we need now. Thank you."

"My family has lived in a shelter for the past two months or so. This shelter is not in the neighborhood where we used to live, but the school district helped with a transportation change so my children did not have to move to a new school. My children have had to adjust to so much that is hard, so it helped a lot for them to stay with their friends at their school."

"I really want to be a taxpayer again. I started a part-time job recently. I hope it will grow into full time. My wife is still looking for a job. She has been trained as a bus monitor, and one day a week she rides to school with our children and stays at school all day to do volunteer work. It is one way for our family to pay back the school system for all you do for us."

"Someday, I will own a house again, and I will be happy to pay property taxes to support our schools. For now, thank you for helping to support our family, and thank you for caring so much about my children. You've done all of this right here. I never had to wait in long lines or fill out endless forms like government sometimes has to require. We obey your rules. We qualify for your extra help now. We could not get through these difficult economic times without a school district that knows that hungry students can't learn."

"For my family and for families like us, thank you very much. I need to leave now and go check on my family. My wife is making sure that the homework for school gets done. My ride from the shelter will be here to pick me up soon. I need to leave. Thank you again."

There is no limit to what grassroots efforts to improve schools can accomplish. From challenging students academically to helping organize life's essentials for students whose families face severe hardships, schools can cause academic learning and can also cause learning of life lessons, such as: in a community, we are in this together.

7

The National Government and State Governments

Candidates for governor of a state and people who actually become governor of a state may promise to be "the education governor." This guarantees that every four years or every eight years, when a new governor takes office, there will be an education reform program introduced by the new governor.

The motives behind the new education reform can range from a genuine effort to improve education to an attempt to reverse prior state laws or regulations that are disagreed with to assertion of political power to attracting votes. States that are doing good work in education may nonetheless be subjected to an education reform movement because the political leadership in the state has decided to advocate reform regardless of current school results but because of possible political results.

It is usual for state governments to have constitutional authority to provide a school system throughout the state. The language in state constitutions may vary, but the impact could be similar to this statement from the Kentucky Constitution, section 183: "The General Assembly shall, by appropriate legislation, provide for an efficient system of common schools throughout the state."

What does the Constitution of the United States of America say about education? Nothing. What authority over education did the nation's brilliant Constitution writers give to the national government when they gathered in 1787 to write the national Constitution? None.

How far must the "necessary and proper" clause of the Constitution be stretched to justify federal government involvement in education? Quite far, farther than the Tenth Amendment to the U.S. Constitution anticipated. The Tenth Amendment states, "The powers not delegated to the United States by the Constitution, nor prohibited by it to the States, are reserved to the States respectively, or to the people."

The word "education" is not included in the United States Constitution. The power over education is not delegated to the United States by the Constitution, nor is the power over education denied to the states by the Constitution. The logical, constitutional conclusion would be that authority for education is reserved to the states or to the people.

The modern reality is inconsistent with the 1787 constitutional wording and with the Tenth Amendment wording as adopted in 1791. What changed? The words of the Constitution did not change. The interpretation of those words, including "necessary and proper" changed. The modern reality must be dealt with, rather than denied or decried.

What is a good way to show the national government that it needs to play a reduced role in education? Get such good results at schools that the national government has to admit that it does not need to get involved.

What is a good way to show state governments that they do not need to impose another political, bureaucratic, systemic, top-down reform of education? Get such good results at schools that the state governments have to admit that no education reform is needed.

How is this done? The Tenth Amendment to the U.S. Constitution ends with two words that answer that question: "the people." Reality is that "the people" at the grassroots level of communities and schools must contend with the political realities of state government authority over schools and national government involvement in schools. This chapter will consider those realities and how to deal with them.

Begin with a speech by a candidate for president. This speech, claimed by the candidate's campaign staff as a major policy address on education to show the voters what this candidate would do about education if the voters elect him as president, is designed to achieve several goals.

Some of those goals are political, and some of those goals are educational. As the reader ponders this speech, consider whether any of the ideas in this speech should be national government issues, and consider what the outcomes could be of implementing these ideas.

Before reading the presidential candidate's speech, analyze this sequence. The national government passes a law about kindergarten through high school education. The national government's Department of Education notifies governors and state departments of education about the new law and all new regulations associated with the law. The state education department in each state has to create new policies and/or regulations.

The state Department of Education informs all local school district superintendents and local school board members about the new law, the new federal regulations, and the resulting state regulations to implement the law. The local school boards then pass policies to implement the new law and the new regulations. School principals are then told all of the requirements of the new law and the new regulations and are told to make all of this happen immediately.

Does that sequence of events appear to anyone as the most efficient, the most effective, and the most sensible way to improve student achievement by causing more and better learning in the educational experience of students? Is there a better way? Yes! Yet in the world of political reality, people who seek to truly improve schools must contend with presidential candidates and with presidents whose confidence in top-down reform is unfounded and whose confidence in bureaucracy defies logic.

"My fellow citizens. This campaign is about the future of our nation, the future of the United States of America. We face many perplexing problems today, but our history shows that when this nation dedicates itself to solving a problem, the results are exemplary."

"When we needed a better transportation system, the national government led the way to build the vital interstate highways. None of us would go back to the old system of two-lane roads."

"When we were losing the space race, the national government led the way with NASA. The goal of getting to the moon and back by the end of the 1960s was set and was reached. The United States inspired mankind with that historic achievement."

"It is time to set new goals and to dedicate this nation to reaching those goals. I speak to you today of our schools and of the overall education system. My conclusion is blunt—our schools are not getting the results that our nation must have. In a global economy, for our nation to complete, we must have workers who have the best education in the world. Our best students and our best schools can compete with any students and any schools in the world. That is not good enough. All of our students and all of our schools must be high quality and must be internationally competitive."

"How will this be done? We must set very exact and very measurable goals. Every student will read at or above grade level. Every student will master math at or above grade level. Every student will have technology skills equivalent to what the workplace requires. Every student will graduate from high school. Every student will have the opportunity to attend college, vocational school, or technical school after graduation from high school."

"How will these goals be reached? I propose a federal government reform of kindergarten through high school. This reform will be built on testing. If a student has mastered the academic work in first grade, she moves to second grade. If a student has not mastered the academic work in first grade, it will be obvious through frequent testing during the first-grade year that the student is not on schedule to succeed."

"Interventions will begin as needed immediately after the first round of tests fairly early in the school year. Those interventions will get the student back on schedule to master all grade-level content by the end of the school year or by the end of an extended school year if more time is needed. Working in very small groups for a few weeks after the regular end of the school year will enable each student to be on schedule and to be fully prepared for the academic work at the next grade level."

"Please notice what I just explained. We are going to eliminate academic failure in our schools. We are going to identify any student, early and often during a school year, who needs additional help. That help will be provided quickly, directly, and individually. No student will fail because no school will fail in its duty to educate each and every student."

"The national government's Department of Education will work closely with the U.S. Congress after our education reform bill is signed into law. Aggressive monitoring by congressional oversight committees combined with thorough monitoring by the Department of Education will assure that all fifty states are in complete compliance with the requirements of our reform. State governments will provide frequent update reports to show statistics based on tests given to all students in each grade and will provide frequent reports on intervention efforts to bring every student up to grade-level performance."

"All states will provide detailed data about high school graduation rates and high school drop-out rates. This data will be provided by county and by school. National government officials from the Department of Education in Washington DC will work with state government officials in all fifty states to take the necessary action with any high school that has less than a 100 percent high school graduation rate after the new reform law has been in effect for five years. School districts that have any underperforming high schools will be subject to strict federal government investigation and will risk losing some federal government education funds."

"There are some other presidential candidates who claim that the national government should reduce its role in education instead of increase its role. Those people must be satisfied with second best. Those people would have lost the space race. Those people would have said that building a national interstate highway system was too much to attempt. Those people have been proven wrong before, and they will be proven wrong again."

"Our national Constitution begins with the inspiring words, 'We, the people of the United States, in order to form a more perfect union.' Our union cannot become more perfect if our educational system is ordinary. Will you join me in forming a more perfect union by building a zero-failure school system throughout this nation? We are Americans. We can do this. We must do this."

A few days after the above speech was made, another presidential candidate addressed the topic of education. Contrast the following speech with the education reform plan presented above.

"My fellow Americans, this election will determine the future of our nation. Our nation has used presidential elections in the past to make national decisions on essential issues and to choose a path of courage rather than a path of inaction."

"When Thomas Jefferson was elected in 1800, when Abraham Lincoln was elected in 1860, when Theodore Roosevelt was elected in 1904, and when Franklin Roosevelt was elected in 1932, our nation defined itself by the decisions made on who our leaders would be and on what our nation would be. We are at such a time with the current presidential election."

"All Americans would agree that we face a long list of problems and challenges. The economy, the national debt, social programs, international unrest, terrorism, crime, health care costs and availability, defense, and energy are among the current issues we must resolve. Add to the list of national concerns the quality of education in this country, but do not add education to the list of problems that should be resolved through the national government."

"Do not interpret this as a lack of concern about education. I was governor of a state for eight years. We made many improvements in the schools of that state during those eight years. Our approach was that education's problems are in schools, so education's solutions must come from the schools. No two schools in our state used the same solutions to address their problems because no two schools had identical problems, people, or perspectives. Every school in our state showed significant student achievement based on annual test scores during those eight years. We got results without increasing the state government bureaucracy in education. We trusted and we empowered local people to solve local problems."

"Also while I was governor, our state attorney general legally challenged some mandates of the United States Department of Education. Our reasoning was that education is a state government responsibility. Our support was the Tenth Amendment to the U.S. Constitution. Our challenge was resolved out of court as the U.S. Department of Education and the U.S. Justice Department agreed to give our state waivers on the mandates we opposed."

"In recent decades, presidents of this country have worked to become the education president. I will not seek that title. I will seek to be the president who removed the federal government bureaucracy from interfering with and from complicating education matters that are resolved much better of, by, and for the people in each state, in each community, and at each school. There are some issues, such as national defense, that the U.S. government can best manage. There are other issues that are much better resolved at the state and local level."

"I trust the people at each school, in each school district, and in each state to care enough about the education of each student to solve the local and state education problems they face. The national government is not the solution to education problems. Teachers, principals, counselors, staff members, parents, guardians, school board members, community members, volunteers, and students are the solutions to education problems. We, the people, can solve these problems."

Which candidate made more sense? Which perspective is more practical and realistic? Which proposal would get more support from voters? Which proposal would get more results for students? Which proposal would have more staying power versus being reformed in a few years? Which proposal would result in more learning being caused in more classrooms? Which proposal makes more sense financially? Which perspective does the reader support?

Quick history reminder: in the late 1950s, the United States fell behind in the space race. The Union of Soviet Socialist Republics launched a satellite, Sputnik, and that nation took an early lead in the space race.

Among the responses by the United States government was a law that would promote math and science education. This was done under the national government's authority to defend the nation. The logic must have been that the United States was behind in the space race because students in the United States were behind in math and science.

By the end of the 1960s, the United States had won the space race as measured by getting to the moon and back home first. The scientists and mathematicians who helped make that space race victory possible were not in kindergarten through high school or in college during the late 1950s and the 1960s after the National Defense Education Act had been passed and implemented. The United States won the space race through a determined commitment to and generous support for the space program, not because math and science instruction changed in the 1960s.

In recent years, new concerns have been expressed about whether students in the United States can compete with students from other nations in math and science. Will the federal government pass a new law, the Interstate Commerce and Education Act, this time using international economic concerns as the justification as in the late 1950s space race and defense concerns were the justification? The Constitution gives Congress authority over interstate commerce and over defense but not over education. Beware of attempts to stretch the Constitution.

Beware, also, of the impracticality of asking the federal government to do what it cannot feasibly accomplish. Education is a national concern, but there is not a one-size-fits-all national government reform of education that can be implemented efficiently and that would be the best solution for every school, for every student, for every community, for every educator.

What can be done at the state government level? Since state governments are authorized by state constitutions to provide an educational system, the issue is not jurisdiction; rather, the issue is what works versus what does not work. Few states would claim to have perfect uniformity throughout the state. There are urban areas and rural areas. There can be manufacturing centers and farming communities.

Geography can create multiple regions within a state. These factors are among the reasons why a state one-size-fits-all solution to education problems or to other problems will encounter the stress test of reality. What's a state government to do?

Listen, listen more, keep listening. Listen to whom? Not so much to the political leaders or the education officials of the other forty-nine states. Of course, know what the other states are doing and be aware of their successes and failures, but use that information judiciously.

Listen to the people of your state. Listen to the voters, taxpayers, parents, guardians, educators, students, business owners, employers, employees, and community leaders, and really hear what they are saying. If you would like to improve education, it is necessary to accurately know what is wrong in education. Ask the people who are face-to-face daily with the process of education. They can tell you what reality is because they deal with reality all day, every day. A state government committee meeting about education is a real meeting, but it may not hear the complete reality about schools unless people who work in those schools are heard.

Before a state considers a massive top-down, political, bureaucratic, systemic reform of education, ask these questions: What happened to the last top-down reform of education? Why was it dismantled? Why did it not live up to the promises made? Why was it rejected a few years after it was approved? What does that reveal about using the state political process to reform education from the top down?

People in your state already know what works in education. Ask them. Perhaps, in your state, awards are given in school districts or statewide to honor the best teachers. Ask those teachers what they know and what they do. Tell all other teachers what those master teachers know and what those master teachers do.

Perhaps, in your state, awards are given to outstanding principals, guidance counselors, superintendents, school board members, and other people involved in education. Ask those people what they know and what they do. What works in education is known and can be communicated. As people hear what works and make necessary adjustments to apply those truths to their unique setting, great results are possible.

Great teachers challenge their students. Great teachers have always challenged their students. Great teachers will always challenge their students. That is a timeless truth in education. There is no need to rethink, "Should we challenge our students?" The answer is forever: yes!

State governments do not need to reform everything in education. If it has been seven years since the last reform in education in a state, the education reform alarm clock need not ring with an insistence that a new reform must be imposed. Listen to people who know education in your state, who care about education in your state, who are impacted by education in your state, and who are impacting education in your state. Their words are much more valuable than the ringing noise of the education reform alarm clock.

I once asked a very successful restaurant entrepreneur what made the difference in his chain of restaurants between those that were most successful and those that were average or unsuccessful. His answer was "standards." He explained that some restaurant workers surpassed every established procedure, policy, and practice. They went above the standards, and their success was superior.

The other restaurants barely met the standards or fell below the standards. Every employee was trained the same way and was trained to know the same skills. Some employees saw the established standards as the peak performance, and if they reached the standards, that was all they did. Other employees set higher standards for themselves than the company set for the workers, and these employees created the best restaurants. The company rewarded superior work and seriously addressed below average work. Employee ideas and concerns were heard, but employee excuses were not tolerated.

In addition to hearing the ideas and concerns of people in a state as they express their thoughts about education, be sure that educators are living up the required standards. This reciprocity can be wholesome and productive. Yes, your concerns and ideas will be heard. Your input will precede any changes. No one person will get every change he or she desires, but every person will be heard. Once the decision is made and the goals are established, everyone is expected to implement the decision and reach the goals. To avoid top-down reform, it is imperative to get bottom-up results.

A state government decided to work with local school districts to get focus group input from teachers, principals, and guidance counselors from every school in the state. This would be a large project, but it was hoped that each school could benefit from the input and that each school district could benefit from the input, in addition to the state government getting frontline ideas and concerns.

At one high school, a group of five teachers, one guidance counselor, and the principal attended the focus group. A central office employee of the school district moderated the discussion. Some of the verbatim comments are below.

Moderator: Thank you for being here today. This is one of several focus groups that will be held at your school. The intention is for your ideas to be part of an overall evaluation of what is working well at your school and of what can be improved. Your school, the school district, and the state government will gain insights about education based on what you say today, so please be open and honest. I have two questions to ask. The first question is: what works best at your school?

Teacher 1: I would say that what works best at this school is our grading scale. We got rid of D grades a few years ago. The lowest D grade was 65 percent, which meant a student did not know 35 percent of the material. We eliminated the D grade, which was 65 percent to 74 percent. Now the lowest C grade is 75 percent, and below that is failing. Students take this seriously, and their work has improved.

Teacher 2: That's a great question. It is so easy to complain and to think of what goes wrong. What's best at this school is our zero-tolerance policy on not doing homework. We used to have students who proudly claimed that they would never do homework. They knew their grade on any homework not done was a zero, but they did not care.

If they failed a class, they knew that they could make it up with an easy two-week computer tutorial. So the rule changed. To qualify for any computer tutorial, a student had to have completed and turned in all homework. Well, turning in homework led to more learning, to better grades, and to fewer students needing the remedial tutorial help. It was good for everyone.

Teacher 3: What's best at this school is that everyone talks to each other. We constantly trade ideas. Teachers post great lesson plans on a sharing website. We find out what is working in an English class and figure out how to apply that in math or science. The teachers sometimes will use a planning period to visit another classroom and get new ideas. So our school has this atmosphere of everyone constantly learning from each other.

One great thing about that is we never have to sit through the typical, awful, irrelevant professional development. We create our own professional development programs with teachers here teaching each other about what works.

Teacher 4: What's best here is that the administrators and counselors are out in the hallways at every class change. No matter where a student is, there is a principal, assistant principal, or counselor in the hall everywhere. This means that very few students are late to class. That helps so much. Class is not interrupted by late students. Plus the public address system is almost never used during classes, so we avoid interruptions like that. It really helps us teach if we have no interruptions.

Teacher 5: What's best at this school is that most of the students do what they are supposed to do most of the time. We reward students a lot. We figured out that a discipline system that punishes students when they misbehave is only half of the process we needed. The other half is to acknowledge and reward students for doing what is right. Not getting punished or staying out of trouble may be enough incentive for some people along with a commitment to doing what is right because it is right, but adding rewards for good behavior is a real personal touch. Everyone likes to be noticed for good work or good behavior.

Guidance counselor: I agree with that. We do reward students to show them what matters most. We noticed years ago that our trophy case was filled with sports trophies, but we are a school. Of course, we like sports, and we get excited about sports, but our real job is education, so our most elaborate celebrations at this school are for academic achievement and for academic improvement.

We like touchdowns, but we love straight-A grades, and we love it when grades go up. Our actions as a faculty and staff show the students what this school is really about, and that includes what we reward, good work and good behavior. When a prom ticket costs $40, but good grades can get you a free ticket, the students take notice.

Principal: What works best at this school is our single-minded dedication to student achievement. Everything we do is with learning in mind. If somebody brings an idea to me or a request to me, my response is, "Who will learn, and what will they learn if we do this?" I do everything I can to base every decision I make on how that decision will impact student learning.

Moderator: When you think of state government or of the local school district, what suggestion would you offer to people who will work there so they can better understand what you need?

Teacher 1: That's easy. Fewer tests. Every year we spend a full week on the tests the state requires. No student is going to be at their best for five consecutive days of testing. Pick out the two or three most important tests, and let's get those done in no more than two school days.

Teacher 2: I think the people who work in the state department of education need to come back and teach every so often. They are so far away in miles and in awareness from what really happens in schools. How can they tell us what to do when they really do not know what we are doing?

Teacher 3: My idea is for the governor, the lieutenant governor, and all of the state legislators to be required to spend three days each year as substitute teachers. They tell us how concerned they are about schools, well, show up. Spending 1 percent of each year in schools would do more good than almost anything else those people could do. They could see for themselves what schools need and what schools do not need.

Teacher 4: I really feel sorry for the school board members because they put in a lot of hours for no pay. I would suggest that changes be made in their duties so they have fewer meetings. That could open some time for them to get into schools and to see what is really going on. I can't imagine that they like all of those meetings.

Teacher 5: My request is that the state education people and the local school district people quit sending us so many e-mails, especially the e-mails that tell us of some Internet video training programs we have to watch again just like we did last year. The e-mails they send that tell us about new rules and regulations that we had no input on are also annoying. It's as if someone in a certain office sends us an e-mail we are supposed to stop everything else we are doing and take care of what they need. I would prefer to concentrate on what my students need.

Guidance counselor: I would ask for the local school board and the state government to realize that a high school of two thousand students needs more than four guidance counselors. Do they really expect me to get to know five hundred students as well as it takes to provide each student with the type of guidance they need?

Principal: School today is different in a lot of ways than school once was. Families have changed. Technology has changed how people live. The economy is different. College costs more than ever, and most of our students are not sure they can afford it. I would ask the powers that be to realize that schools face some difficulties and needs today that are new. When we ask for more help it is because we need more help.

Multiply that focus group times ten, and the input from that high school expands. Multiply that focus group to include similar groups from all schools in this school district, and the local authorities have a new opportunity to respond to the realities their colleagues are telling them about. Multiply that focus group by all of the schools in the state, and the state government has been given a more thorough and a more realistic perspective on schools than is otherwise available.

Any actions taken by local school boards or the state government based on these grassroots focus groups can surpass in quality, in efficiency, and in effectiveness what any top-down reform could imagine. Better yet, local school boards and state governments could work with each school so the problems confronted by and the solutions implemented at each school really work for each school.

Why would they work? Because they are locally realistic, locally identified, locally committed to, locally bought into, locally useful, and locally meaningful. School improvement efforts that are of, by, and for the grassroots local level are much more likely to succeed than top-down reforms, which originate far from the grassroots local level.

"But the national government is offering amazing financial incentives. They have several billion dollars in money that will go to the states that apply for it and are chosen. There are several actions they expect the states to take if they get the money. So if states will change their school systems the way the federal government wants them to, they could get this extra funding."

Perhaps what the federal government is motivating states to do, in pursuit of being chosen for the financial aid, is not what the states think is actually in the best interests of education for each of those states. Why let the federal government's financial carrot subject your state to the federal government stick of its rules, regulations, and compliance obligations? Also, beware of making costly education changes that the federal government pays for this year but may not pay for in later years.

It may take some extra courage to say "no" to the federal government's financial incentives that are awarded to states that create education reform plans that the federal government pays for because the reform plans are consistent with what the federal government is seeking to get states to do. Is it wise to let the source of about 8 percent of education funding—the federal government—control much more than 8 percent of what schools do and how schools do that? The economics warning is "buyer beware." The education warning is "grant applicant or government beneficiary beware."

As society faces increasingly difficult problems, as the pace of life increasingly accelerates, as economic limits mount, as demographic changes continue, more problems that state governments have previously dealt with and resolved may be pushed to the national government. This trend is of concern and need not happen.

States can and should let the national government know that more and better education improvement ideas come from local schools than can ever come from Washington DC. Then states should show the national government, by example, that deference to the local schools is grassroots democracy and grassroots reality. The states must demand much from the local school districts. The local school districts must meet or surpass state demands.

The states must convince the national government that the local schools are doing or can do their jobs and deserve to be allowed to work and to improve without federal government intervention.

Educators may vary in their thoughts about how helpful federal government involvement in education is. Some educators may think that states overlooked issues, which then had to be taken to the federal government level. Nonetheless, when the national government passes laws that require all schools to conform to specific requirements, states and localities lose the flexibility they can need to resolve matters that are unique to each state and to each locality. The same caution is valid for states—when all schools are required to conform to specific requirements, localities lose the flexibility they can need to resolve matters that are unique to each locality.

We move now from the national government and state government arenas to the role that businesses and business advocacy groups can play in grassroots efforts to improve education.

8

Businesses and Business Advocacy Groups

"We need employees who are willing to work, really work. We need employees who accept responsibility, actually who seek and welcome responsibility. We need employees who are on time, who are polite, who do not make excuses, and who do more than is required. We need employees who obey rules, follow directions, and who never goof off. We do not expect perfection, but we need employees who make very few mistakes and who correct their mistakes quickly."

The school board members were listening intently as a group of six local business owners spoke on behalf of the local chamber of commerce. The idea was for the school board to be updated on what local employers needed. The hope was that schools would evaluate their overall curriculum and extracurricular activities to ensure that students were developing the work skills that employers needed.

The first person to address the school board manages a retirement facility where older residents live in various levels of independence or assistance. High school students are often hired to work in the dining room at this facility. Serving supper on weeknights and serving all meals on weekends means that the students must have the work ethic, the character, and the people skills that the manager itemized for the school board. Five more local business owners or executives also spoke to the school board.

"I own three fitness clubs. We pride ourselves on being very family friendly. Some of our employees began coming to our workout centers when they were children. We have unique activities for all ages, including closely supervised play for very young children and closely guided exercise for older children and younger teenagers. Some high school students work for us now, and they are excellent employees. I keep in touch with the guidance counselors at the high schools. They help me find the right people for part-time jobs."

"Who are those people? I start with their attendance records. The cutoff is 98 percent attendance. If you miss more than 2 percent of the school days, we do not interview you. I need people who consistently show up. I also look at their on-time results. If you are late to school or to classes more than 2 percent of the time, we do not interview you. Then I ask about grades. If you made any C grades, we do not interview you. That process always provides excellent employees. We pay them above minimum wage, so we insist on above minimum qualifications."

"I manage and own an upscale restaurant. I also own three pizza places and two frozen yogurt places. I supervise hiring for all of the six locations. I look for the same characteristics in my employees who are high school age at all of the locations. Are you trustworthy? If you have ever been suspended from school, you do not work for me. Are you reliable and dependable? Letters of recommendation are not enough. I need to talk with people who know you."

"Are you stretching yourself too far with a part-time job? You will show me your report card, and it has to be over a B average, or you do not work until the grades are back up. Do you have great people skills? We treat our customers like they are the royal family, and I need to know you have superior manners. So I hope the schools are teaching skills and characteristics like these because that is what my businesses need."

"I own a clothing store. I need employees who understand the math part of a business. I need them to realize that they are expected to sell enough clothes to pay their hourly wage, to pay the store's hourly costs, and to help us make a profit. I show them the costs of doing business, and we put that in terms of cost per hour to be open as a store. Their work must generate the sales that more than cover those costs. They usually seem stunned by the numbers. I guess they never thought about what it takes to make a business profitable. I hope that the schools can teach some practical math skills along with all of the sophisticated math and advanced math."

"Algebra and calculus are good, but please be sure that students can do practical business math. They also need to know the math of personal finance. They wonder why their paychecks have several deductions. They also wonder why their paychecks evaporate as they buy new cell phones or go out with friends for entertainment. Please be sure they learn the real math of running a business, of balancing a checkbook, of staying on a budget. How will they pay for college if they are unaware of money math?"

"I own a cleaning service. I have many full-time employees. Some have worked for me a long time. They clean residences and businesses. I also hire some high school students who work for my company in the early evening when we clean office buildings. Here's what I need from the schools. Help your students learn that work is work. There are no second chances for our company. We have competitors. Clients can decide to not renew our contract."

"I look for employees who take the initiative. I look for people who clean a place so thoroughly that nothing more could be done to make it cleaner. At school, let students know that due dates are real. Don't give them credit for late work. My company loses business and money if I get a call from a client who was not satisfied. I have to send someone back to that place and correct what should have been done right in the first place."

"I manage a large landscape center, and we also have a lawn cutting service. In the summer when school is out, I sometimes hire older high school students to cut lawns. I hire fewer high school students than I used to because so many would quit after a few weeks. This is hot, hard work. Now, the ones I do hire almost never quit. Why? Because I learned who to hire. I look for students who do well in school, who behave in school, and who are involved in something."

"The athletes and the marching band members usually make good employees. So do the students who are in lots of clubs or who were elected to school offices. Those students understand more about responsibility and work. So I hope the schools will create more opportunities for every student to get involved in a sport, or a club, a musical group, theater, the school newspaper, or something like that. The transition from those duties to a job seems to be smoother than if a student never had those extra duties at school."

One school board member had a question for the panel of business owners and managers. "Perhaps the schools could use your help. Imagine the benefits to everyone if each school in our school district could be adopted or mentored or partnered with, choose whatever description you like, by a business in this community. People from the business could visit math classes and teach about business math. People from the businesses could tell students how to apply for jobs and how to interview for jobs. The businesses could help schools publicize events. If the business was replacing old equipment, it could give the old equipment to their partner school. Could something like this be done?"

The fitness club owner replied. "That is a big idea. Could the six of us meet with you or whoever you select for the schools and see if we can make that happen?" A meeting was scheduled, the plan was developed, the six businesses partnered with six schools to test the idea for a year, the idea worked, and eventually every school had one or two businesses partners. The partnership and the results were symbiotic, were beyond all expectations, and were very grassroots. It took a lot of work to establish and maintain the partnerships. That work, everyone agreed, was worth it. It took no laws, regulations, policies, or taxes to establish and to maintain the partnerships.

What would be involved in establishing a school and business partnership program if it were initiated by the national government or by a state government? The president or a governor would give a major education policy speech to a business convention or conference. The speech would introduce the concepts that would be included in the "Business and Education Partnership for Educational Support and Innovation Act." The news media would report on the proposal. People would take sides on the proposal as the debate began.

Legislative hearings would be called as scripted input was provided to legislators. Business groups, education groups, lobbyists, and citizens would be heard from. A legislative committee would approve the bill, and it would be voted on. Then the other legislative chamber would consider the bill. Then the legislative branch completes approval of the bill, with many changes made versus the original and with a few additional topics included, such as a new mandate for more reading testing and a new mandate for all students to be informed annually about safe use of the Internet.

The bill is signed into law, and the Department of Education, which will monitor implementation of the law and compliance with the law, will write the regulations that show specifically what is required of school districts and of schools. The regulations will be posted for comment, and there will be many comments because regulations can be confusing, complex, and subject to interpretation.

Finally, the regulations are approved, and schools have one year to show substantial progress toward implementing the law and two years to fully implement the law. Legislative oversight via committees getting testimony from Department of Education officials will be continuous through the two-year initial implementation phase. Every school and every school district will submit an annual report to show their compliance with the law.

During that two-year period, a new president or a new governor is elected. This new executive supports the law but has many changes to propose that would modify the law. The process begins again just as schools are implementing the original law. They will be told what to stop doing and what to start doing. Such is the process, and such is the reality of top-down, political, bureaucratic education reform.

There are some issues in our nation and in our states that absolutely must go through the political process always. The slow, cumbersome political process has built-in delays along with checks and balances to help participants reach a reasonable decision.

What does the reader think? Is a business and school partnership implemented better when it is established through a grassroots effort or when it is established through a political reform? What are the most important differences in the two approaches? If grassroots efforts lead the way, could there be less justification or rationalization for and less frequency of top-down reforms?

Do people who own, manage, or work in a business think about their daily duties the same way that people who work in education think about their duties? Can and should a school be run like a business? Can what causes a business to succeed be applied to education to equally cause schools to succeed? Are there some inherent differences between businesses and schools that necessitate some awareness that some ideas and actions that work in one would not work in the other? The following story will consider these questions.

BUT THAT ALWAYS WORKS FOR OUR BUSINESS

"When sales slow down, we get more aggressive. We offer deals. Buy one get one free. We have sales—10 percent off everything. We have big events where a famous athlete is at the store one day, and people can get a picture made and an autograph. We give coupons for discounts when you return within a certain time. We give employees an instant bonus when a customer says something good about the employee to a manager. We increase our advertising on television, radio, and in the newspaper. When sales are strong, we do not rest. We still offer deals and incentives. We never stop trying to build our business, and our experience is that customers will come if you give them enough reasons to come."

That business owner was talking to a high school principal who quickly replied, "We cannot say to a student that an A grade on one test will get them a free grade of A on the next test. Earn one A, get one A free will not work in school. We can't give discounts. Do all the homework assigned today, and get a 50 percent reduction in the amount of homework assigned tomorrow. I can't say to the first fifty students who show up one day that they get a discount so their next tardy to class is erased like you can to the first fifty shoppers that they get an early bird discount. You and I have a lot of similar goals for education, I'm sure, but we cannot always use the same techniques or tactics."

The business owner was intrigued with the statement about goals, but she still hoped that some business methods could work in education. She responded, "I understand. Our work is different, but we have some similar goals. My business gets the best ideas from employees and from customers. I never pay some consultant to come study my business and tell me what to do. They would come in for two days, charge a fortune, hand me a fairly general report, and then leave town. I constantly seek ideas, input, criticism, and good news from our employees and from our customers."

"We reward employees for their suggestions, any suggestion. We give extra rewards when their suggestion is implemented and gets good results. We want them to constantly think about what we can do better. My employees and I talk to customers all the time. There is a lot of competition in the sporting goods business. Our store has been family owned and operated for forty-six years. The people in this community know us, and we know them."

"I keep in close touch with the employees and the customers, so it is more than just a place to work or to shop. It's a place where talents are developed, and customer needs are met. How do you listen to your employees and to your customers?"

Interesting question. The principal paused, pondered, and said, "The truth is that I have no employees who work for me. All of us are employees of the school district. Still, I have supervisory duties, and I evaluate everyone at this school. Yes, I listen to the people who work here, but I could listen more. I'm sure that the teachers express a lot of frustrations and talk about successes in the faculty work room, but I'm never there. I get stuck in the office too much. I do need to hear more from everyone at school."

"Now, do I have any customers? Not exactly like you do, but taxpayers, parents, guardians, and students are all sort of in that category. I can't give all of those groups everything they ask for, but I can do more customer service and see if they are satisfied with this school or not. I could build upon what they tell me is good, and I could investigate what they tell me is bad. I could follow up with them so they know their input was taken seriously. Could that apply a business approach to education?"

The store owner smiles, "Yes. That can work. Now, about those goals we share. I have wondered if what you need students to do at school is similar to what I need employees to do at work. I need employees who are on time, who follow instructions, who learn all about the business so they can answer all questions from customers, who know where everything is in the store, who are polite, who stay very informed about sports, including local teams at high schools or colleges or youth leagues, and I need people who really like to work. Does that describe a good employee and a good student?"

The principal was very interested. "Yes. Yes, it does. I would love for our students and our teachers to hear from you. Let's figure out a way that my school and your business can team up. You could find some great part-time employees in our student body. Our students could see that their work at school connects with work at a business. Our teachers would have the benefit of your stature in the community when they tell students to follow your advice. Can we do something together?"

That question was easy to answer. "Yes. Absolutely yes. I'd rather help you improve your school with some of my time and effort than see school taxes go up. I might be optimistic, but if your school and my business can create a strong partnership, just imagine what could be accomplished. The school board will ask you what in the world is going on at your high school. They'll know it was not more money from them. So, sure, let's get to work and see what can be done."

"You know, I graduated from your high school twenty-four years ago, and then I studied business in college right here at the university. This will be a great homecoming for me. I might be able to get some of the university professors and coaches to help us, maybe some college students, too. Let's get started. Creative ideas like this usually work in our business; now it can work in business and school. I knew we could find something in common."

Business and education can reason together but will not think identically. Common ground and shared goals can be found. The purpose of a school is to cause learning, and while the purpose of a business is different, there are times when a business needs its employees to learn and when a business needs current or potential customers to learn about the business. Educators could offer ideas to the business about various methods that cause learning. Businesses can offer ideas to educators about various methods that motivate employees and that increase satisfaction of customers. Everyone wins.

When state political leaders make the plans for a new top-down, political, bureaucratic, systemic reform of education, it is likely that they will seek to build widespread support for the reform. Among those whose support will be sought are statewide business advocacy groups. The motives to support the reform can range from sincere agreement with the content of and comfort with the political procedure involved with a top-down reform to the practical politics of supporting a plan that is likely to be implemented, so you do not get left out.

The business advocacy groups—chambers of commerce, associations of industries, business coalitions, and others—may see the politics of reform more than they see the content of reform. This could come from these groups dealing with political realities every day while they deal with education less often. Analyze the content of the education reform as thoroughly as you would analyze the content of a proposal for your business. Be skeptical, demanding, critical, and curious as you search for what is best rather than what is politically popular, trendy, or advantageous.

Consider the executive board of a business advocacy group as it hears and then responds to a top-down education reform proposal presented by the lieutenant governor of the state.

"We need your help and your support. The governor is determined to fix education in this state. According to most measurements in education, this state is ranked thirtieth to fortieth, unless you look at high school dropouts, and we are tenth. That is tenth most dropouts. Small steps will not be enough. It is time for drastic, sweeping reform of education. Our plan has three key parts. We are completing the support documentation for the plan, but I wanted to give you an early preview because your opinions are respected and because your support will be vital."

"First, we intend to do away with the old process of students pass from one grade to the next grade because they attended enough days and make passing grades. Every student in every grade will have to demonstrate on an end-of-year test that the academic basics of the grade have been mastered. Mastered means 80 percent correct on the end-of-year test. If you make 80 percent or better, you move on to the next grade. If you make under 80 percent, you do online tutorial work and then retake the end-of-year test; only, it is a different version of the test you took originally. This approach, we are convinced, will move our students and our state up into the top ten nationally."

"Second, we are going to drastically change the ways that people become certified to teach. As it is now, people usually earn their teaching certification as part of their college education or as part of their graduate school education. There are many people in our society who have a college degree, who have career experience outside of education, and who could be excellent teachers. We intend to welcome these people to the profession of education."

"Our state's Department of Education has created an amazing online instructional program that would grant a college graduate with five years of work experience a temporary two-year teaching certificate. If the teaching work done during the two years of that certification meets all required standards of our state's two-year internship program for all new teachers, the person would be given permanent certification. Schools can benefit from an influx of new talent and diverse talent."

"Third, far too many school buildings in this state are old and need substantial renovation. Local school districts are having trouble obtaining the funds needed to modernize school buildings. Schools waste money on old energy systems. Schools use marker boards at a time when every other part of society uses electronic screens. School buildings are closed when the weather is too bad for buses to be on the road, but if school buildings are updated with sufficient technology, teachers can provide Internet lessons, assignments, and instructions, so education continues even when the weather is bad."

"The first and second parts of this plan have minimal costs contrasted with the very costly third part of the plan. We propose that the state sales tax be increased by an additional 1 percent. We also will apply the sales tax to various services that have not been taxed to date—from dry cleaning to car repair, from lawyer fees to funeral services, from accounting work to some medical services. Our economy more and more is a service economy, and our tax system needs to reflect that change."

"Nobody likes tax increases, but we have to be prepared to lose the next election in order to do what is bold, courageous, necessary, and overdue. Businesses will be concerned about having to collect a higher tax from every customer. Businesses that have never had their services taxed before will be especially concerned about this change. We need your assistance and involvement to help businesses understand why these changes in education and in taxation are necessary."

"Now, please share with me your questions and your concerns." Seven of the board members responded quickly to the lieutenant governor.

Member 1: That is a bold plan. Do you think it might be too bold? Maybe do parts one and two now, but wait on part three. There is never a good time to raise taxes, but there are tolerable times and bad times. This is a bad time. If you take 1 percent more from families who are struggling to make ends meet, their struggle will be worse. Businesses can't lose customers. Many businesses are barely staying open as it is. A higher sales tax, just that 1 percent increase, will mean some customers buy less, and some customers will just stop going to some businesses. Do your test plan, and your teacher plan, but all of that new taxing and renovation needs to wait.

Member 2: I'm not real impressed with parts one and two. Maybe you could show us how things like those reforms have worked in other states. You said the students do remedial work online, but we know that some families do not have the Internet. If a student scores a 50 percent and does the remedial work online and then scores an 80 percent, can they keep doing that year after year? I can just imagine some students who goof off never intending to do the work that prepares them to pass the exam. Then they just coast through the online stuff and pass the test. They learned how to beat the system more than they learned any school subject.

Member 3: We have been through this before with other governors. Don't you remember that huge education reform from ten or twelve years ago? Taxes went up for that one. Now, most of that reform is gone because it did not get instant results or some new idea came along or the people who supported that reform are no longer in office. Some of your ideas sound interesting, and they might work, but how long would they last? I think it will be difficult to persuade people to get serious about this plan when they were promised ten years ago that the education problems were going to be solved with everything we supported back then.

Member 4: Where did these ideas come from? Are these the best of the best ideas from other states? Did your political advisors get these ideas from successful candidates they help in other states? Did teachers and principals and superintendents help create these ideas in your plan? Were any college professors from this state involved in making these plans for education reform? Businesspeople like facts. What facts can you give us that prove the three actions you suggest are going to work?

Member 5: We need evidence. Maybe you brought books for us to read. Maybe your staff has compiled the facts. Of course, all of us are for better schools. Of course, we are not satisfied with our state being ranked low in education. The problem I have with your plan is how do we know it is the best plan? What evidence shows that we are better off using this plan than any other plan? Or, for that matter, how do we know that your plan will be better than what is being done in schools now?

Member 6: If we sound skeptical, it is because our experience tells us to ask a lot of questions. Our businesses get presented with ideas every day. We say "no" to most of them. The ones we most seriously consider are the plans that match our business goals. So that is my question. What is the goal you are seeking to reach? How will you know if you reach the goal? If our state moves up from thirty-third in some education measurement to twenty-ninth, is that success? Would you have reached your goal then?

Member 7: We realize that this plan is still being developed. I think your schedule is to make a public announcement of your plan in a few weeks. Our comments are generally telling you that you need very convincing evidence for whatever you end up proposing. Also, we are telling you that this is a really bad time to ask for a tax increase, so beware of that. I would encourage you to look for revenue neutral ways to improve education.

I mean, find ways to improve schools without having to spend more money. If a restaurant spends money to replace the furniture, and now the chairs are really comfortable, but the food is bad, few customers, if any, will come back just to sit in more comfortable chairs. So, figure out what is most important in schools, and then figure out the most practical way to get better results for that most important goal. When you have the final version of your plan prepared, along with all the evidence to support it, let's meet again. Any other comments?

Member 8: I used to be a teacher years ago. I loved teaching. Then our triplets were born. How could I put them through college on a teacher's pay? My wife really wanted to be a stay-at-home mom. I changed jobs soon after the triplets were born. They are in college now. The company I work for helped make that possible with my salary, bonus, and with scholarships for children of employees.

Here's my point about your plan. About twenty years ago, when I was in my third year of teaching, there was a huge statewide reform of education. I remember how concerned and angry the teachers and the principals were because they had no input in the plan. What a mistake. Why try to reform education without input from educators, the people who have to make the plan work? So be sure you give every teacher and principal and everyone else at schools a chance to be heard. Do the same with families and with all taxpayers.

One other idea. Don't reinvent education. School reforms come and go. Ask any person what was best about their education, and you will never hear about reforms. You will hear about great teachers. Concentrate on getting more and more great teaching in every classroom, and the results will be everything you are looking for and will probably cost less, too.

What will the lieutenant governor report to the governor about this meeting with the business leaders? What will the final version of the governor's education plan include and not include? Is it possible that there will not be an education reform plan proposed by the governor? Could the governor consider another approach to improving schools? What could that approach be, and how would the governor find out about it?

In several large cities in the state where the governor was working on the above explained education reform plan, there were advertising clubs. People who worked in advertising, promotion, marketing, and public relations joined these clubs for business networking reasons and for pleasant social occasions.

The clubs were known for making themselves available as idea factories. Nonprofit groups in the state could attend an advertising club meeting, describe the goals of their group, and then hear ideas that were offered free for the taking as a public service of the advertising club.

In one city, a school superintendent asked the advertising club to devote a meeting to brainstorming ideas to improve education. The one restriction, given financial realities, was that the ideas had to be about innovations that required little or no money. The club was delighted to accept this offer. The ideas were presented in rapid succession after a short statement to the advertising club members by the superintendent, who summarized current successes and current problems in the school district. The ideas from advertising club members included the following:

1. Use volunteers to supervise school buildings on Saturdays so students can use the library and computer labs.
2. Have some teachers work Tuesday through Saturday so they can provide remedial work or accelerated work on Saturdays. They could help students get caught up or they could have new opportunities for talented students.
3. Rent school buildings in the summer so the schools make money and people have more activities.
4. Have college professors come teach some classes to high school juniors and seniors to show them what is going to be different in college.

5. Sell the naming rights to high school athletic facilities.
6. Give every teacher the telephone and computer capability in their classroom to instantly contact the family of any student who is misbehaving.
7. Use the closed-circuit television systems in schools to advertise classes, clubs, and volunteer opportunities. Some students do not know everything available at school.
8. Have chefs from local restaurants come work with the cafeteria staff at schools to fix fancy meals.
9. Reward more students. Get businesses to donate prizes so students can get rewarded for good work.
10. Some local businesses need employees in the summer. Put those businesses in touch with teachers who need summer employment.
11. Have school all over town. Why does school have to happen only at school? Arrange for an elementary school teacher to take her class for a field day to a local museum. They can do all of their learning work at the museum and see how all of their subjects relate to the displays at the museum.
12. Have senior citizens come to school and tell students about the events of their lifetime as a way to learn history.
13. Have school and business partnership days. Some employees of a business come to school to do volunteer work one day. After school, students, faculty, and staff are welcome at the business for discounts and deals.
14. Get businesspeople to become an honorary boss of a class. The class members are told what they have to do in their job as a student. The students who do the best work get rewarded by their volunteer boss.
15. There are concerts, theatrical events, lectures, and other events in town that are not sold out. Arrange for remaining unsold tickets to be given to or sold at a big discount to students and educators.
16. Do more with local cable television. Schools could have their own channel. News, instruction, educational documentaries, and helpful information could be on the channels.
17. Have judges hold real or mock juvenile court hearings at a school. Resolve the confidentiality issues so students can know what a courtroom process looks like and feels like.
18. Have more contests where students create radio, television, or Internet advertisements on important topics, such as not smoking or not dropping out of school. Broadcast on local media the winning advertisements.
19. Get lots of businesses to give honor roll discounts. Create an honor roll card, which students earn for their grades and which can be used for discounts at participating businesses.

20. There are many people who have retired from their business careers but who have knowledge, talent, time, and skills. Recruit these people to be mentors and volunteers in schools. They could work individually, under proper supervision, with students who need extra help and with students who seek extra challenges. They could work in the summer with students who are not quite ready to move to the next grade but, with a month of individual summer help, could become fully ready to move up.
21. Create trade days where a businessperson comes to teach classes in school and the regular teacher goes to work for the day in the businessperson's workplace. This could help schools and businesses better understand each other.
22. Some businesses have surplus supplies, furniture, materials, or products. These things sit in storage closets or warehouses. Match these businesses with schools that could use the surplus, and arrange for donations.
23. Get a law passed that says if you worked in banking, for example, for ten years and would like to become a high school business and economics teacher, you may apply for the job. No guarantees of getting hired to teach, but your ten years of experience and any four-year college degree will enable you to apply for the job and be considered for the job.
24. Work with technology companies that are always creating new products and electronic breakthroughs to test their products in the schools at no cost to the school. The technology company can find out how good their new product is, and schools can use the new technology for educational purposes.
25. Recruit retired construction workers who used to work for local construction companies to volunteer their time to help with doing minor remodeling or repairs at schools. They could probably help with larger projects as advisors to school officials who have not had big construction projects at their school before.

Some of those twenty-five ideas are better than others. Some of those twenty-five ideas are more likely to succeed than others. Some of those ideas are more practical than others. Some of those ideas cost no money while others have some expenses. Which of those ideas could create the most school improvement? Which of those ideas could cause the most and the best learning? Which of those ideas could be put together with a grassroots school improvement plan that gets better results than a top-down, political, bureaucratic, mandated education reform could get?

Businesses and business advocacy groups have quite a stake in the quality of schools. Being in schools, listening to people in schools, and creating partnerships with schools can help make businesses and business advocacy groups part of grassroots school improvement efforts, which get results.

Businesses, business advocacy groups, and schools can team up in personal, highly creative, highly productive, and often low-cost ways to improve schools. Contrast that with what usually happens with top-down education reform. Which approach has more promise and more appeal?

9

Students

"My name is Jason Bradley. I am a senior in high school. I have been going to school for 13 years. I never liked school, and I never learned a lot until tenth grade. Up until then, I just got by. I never failed a grade, and I never failed a class, but it was really unusual for me to do great work. I got by."

"My parents always told me that I could do better. It's not that school was so difficult; actually, it was usually easy. I just did not see any reason to work super hard. I was going to graduate and get a job and live happily ever after."

"I do not know if that plan would have worked or not because everything, I mean everything, changed when I was in tenth grade. I had no big plans when I came back to school for tenth grade. For all I knew, it would be just another year of making C grades and an occasional B, being with my friends, and getting old enough to have a driving permit. One teacher had other plans for her students, and I happened to be one of those students."

"Mrs. Christie Matthews was new to our high school that year. She was not new to teaching. She had been a middle school teacher for ten years or so in another town. She and her family moved to our town, and she was hired to teach tenth-grade world history and eleventh-grade United States history. As you might imagine, Mrs. Matthews was my teacher in tenth grade and in eleventh grade."

"From the very first day of our world history class, Mrs. Matthews was the most energetic and enthusiastic teacher I had ever seen. I wondered why she got so excited about all of those old civilizations and old events. She told me that history taught us everything we need to know about how to live. She said history showed every possible mistake people could make and how to avoid those mistakes now. She said history showed many successes and how to be successful. She was certain that, if you understood history, you gave yourself a huge advantage. I decided I wanted that advantage."

"She made us read and read, but the books actually were interesting. She gave us lots of tests, but they were different. They were not just questions to see what you remember, but they were questions that made you apply history to real stuff going on now. That was a new way of thinking for me."

"Mrs. Matthews had us doing something different every day. One day in U.S. history class, our assignment was to research the history of the career we wanted to go into. If you wanted to be a dentist, you researched way back to earlier centuries to see the awful equipment that was used and then how things changed. Well, I was always sort of interested in airplanes, so for that assignment I researched the history of aviation with the idea of being a pilot. It was amazing. People have been trying to fly for centuries. I had no idea."

"Then in the twentieth century, planes really took off—clever choice of words, 'took off'—which was the type of creative writing Mrs. Matthews liked to see us use. Oh, yeah, I started reading a lot on my own about planes, about companies that build planes, about famous pilots in wars, about the career of being a commercial pilot, and about how to get the training needed to have a license to fly a plane. As a gift for graduating from high school, my parents are paying for me to take basic flight instruction."

"My grades improved, not just in my classes with Mrs. Matthews, but in all of my classes. I thought about school differently. Mrs. Matthews always challenged us to be scholars. She loves that word, 'scholar.' Nobody ever had told me that I could be a scholar. I decided to give it a try, and now, well, now I am on my way to college. I will study aviation. I will be a pilot."

"My parents sent me to a junior aviator camp last summer. It was not just a camp you pay for, and you get to go. I had to qualify for this camp. They looked at my grades and said my high school grades showed a huge improvement in my sophomore and junior years. They said my freshman year grades were not good enough for camp admission, but I had improved enough to meet their requirements. Mrs. Matthews is why I improved that much."

"So I am really glad to be part of this teacher recognition program today. Mrs. Christie Matthews is the teacher who made the biggest difference in my education. I hope that when she retires, she travels a lot and that I get to be the pilot of the plane she travels on at least once. I would like for her to see the person she helped me become."

Mrs. Matthews inspired Jason, challenged Jason, taught Jason in ways that caused learning. More than ever in his career as a student, Jason worked. Among the contributions that students can make in their own education is to do the work, all of the work, all of the time, completely and correctly, on time. Doing more work than is required is even better.

It is timely to ask, what motivated Christie Matthews to teach with such energy, creativity, enthusiasm, high standards, and high impact? Was her work due to the mandates of a top-down, political, bureaucratic, systemic education reform? Was her work due to her own grassroots school improvement plan, which she brought to her classroom daily based on promises she made to herself years ago about the type of teacher she would be? Consider those two questions, and determine which answer is more reasonable.

Now read the following statement from a high school senior, and conclude whether this statement is likely to be made.

"My name is Roberta Aguilar. I will graduate from high school soon. I want to thank the governor of the state, the legislators of this state, the state board of education, the state Department of Education, the superintendent of my school district, and the school board of my school district. Eight years ago, all of those people passed an education reform law, and they wrote many regulations to put that law into practice."

"That law required students to take many more tests. I have learned so much about test-taking strategies. I do not know what job that has prepared me for, but when I find a job that requires workers to take a lot of tests, I will be ready for that job."

"The new law also required that our teachers attend many full-day professional development programs during the school year. My teachers were absent a lot to attend these training programs, so we had a lot of substitute teachers. Classes are always easier with substitute teachers, so thank you for reducing my stress level of having to work hard every day."

"The new law also said it was illegal to drop out of high school at age sixteen or seventeen. A student had to be eighteen years old to drop out. That meant some of my friends stayed in school for another year or two and then dropped out. I got to see those friends at school for all that time, and we enjoyed being together."

"That new law apparently changed the topics that teachers taught. There were things called 'academic measures' in every subject and every grade. The teachers had to emphasize this long list of academic measures. There was never any time for anything else because all of those new tests were based on the academic measures. We memorized a lot. We are well prepared for jobs that need workers to memorize a lot of stuff. I'm not sure what those jobs are, so I hope you can tell me."

"Thank you for letting me be taught by so many new, young teachers right out of college. They are so cool. They are smart, and they know everything about technology. Many of the older teachers retired because the new law was so different and changed everything. I know that some of those more experienced teachers were among the best, but it must have been time for them to retire; although, I heard that most of them went to work at private schools. I never knew exactly why."

"I will be in college next year, but I have to take a catch-up math class and a catch-up English class. Two years ago, when all of the tests changed, it made our test scores really strange, so my scores on those new tests showed I went backwards in math and English. I think the test change messed up everything. I kept learning math and English, but the new test said I went backward. Why did the test system change?"

"So, that big education reform law really shook up schools. I sometimes feel like I was part of the generation of students you experimented on with that new law. Do you think the experiment was a success or not?"

What answers would be given if high school students were asked the question, "What should be done to improve your school?" Please add to the following list:

1. Not so much homework.
2. Better food in the cafeteria.
3. More time between classes.
4. More variety of classes so we don't keep taking the same kind of stuff.
5. Make the place safer. Things get stolen all the time.
6. Get the teachers to quit using all of those silly worksheets. We had enough of that in middle school.
7. Get the teachers to use more worksheets. We know how to do those, and they are not confusing.
8. We need more parking places.
9. We need more college classes that we can take now to count for high school credit and college hours.
10. Do something about the students who act up all the time in classes and who start fights. How can the rest of us concentrate and feel safe with all of that stuff going on?
11. Some teachers grade really hard, and some teachers grade really easy. I wish everyone graded the same. Then I would always know what to expect.
12. Why can't I go to vocational school as a ninth grader? I don't need more of these same classes. I need to work on car repair. I'm going to own a car repair shop someday, so let me work on car repair now. Why make me wait until I'm a junior in high school to take vocational classes?
13. Could we please have other languages to study? French and Spanish are not bad, but Chinese and Arabic would be interesting too.
14. Quit telling us to read books. Everything we do, except at school, is electronic and online. Why are schools so far behind?

15. Get rid of snow days. The city does not close down when it snows. If you cancel school, we just go spend the day at the mall, or we ask for extra hours at our jobs. If people stay home when it snows, that's up to them, but let the rest of us stay on schedule, especially seniors who need to graduate on time, not two weeks later because of ten snow days to make up.
16. Tell us more about college when we are in ninth grade and tenth grade. If I had known more about what colleges require, I would have done things differently.
17. Have more sports and more clubs. Have some sports for people who are not superstar athletes but who just like to play.
18. Don't start school so early in the morning.
19. Make our school bigger. There is no room in the halls to get anywhere. Everything is way too crowded.
20. The dress code is too strict. Give us some freedom.
21.

22.

Schools cannot give students everything they want or ask for. Schools can listen to students and filter out the ideas that will not work or that are contrary to the school's goals, objectives, mission, and purpose. The student perception of school is very important to understand. Some ideas from students can be implemented while others must be rejected. There is much learning that can occur in the process of being heard, being taken seriously, and working to advocate your ideas.

What would students say that the purpose of a school is? Would they say "to cause learning"? Consider the following answers to that question from some middle school students, and then add to the list:

1. To get us ready for high school.
2. To get us ready for eighth grade so we can then go to high school.
3. Isn't school supposed to get us ready for our jobs?
4. It's just the place where we go. What else would children do?
5. To make us do what the teachers tell us to do. To behave. To follow rules.
6. To make us learn stuff, school stuff, and how to get along with people and, I guess, how to make friends.
7. To keep us busy all day so we stay out of trouble.
8. To teach us all the stuff we are supposed to learn at school.

9. School is where children go so their parents can go to work. Yeah, we learn and stuff, but it just keeps us under control.
10. To show us how to grow up and, you know, be mature.
11. It's not the purpose, but the best part is seeing my friends.
12.

13.

The student perspective on school is not identical to the perspective of parents, guardians, educators, and other adults. How can students become part of grassroots efforts to improve schools if school improvement to a student looks completely different from how school improvement looks to an adult?

Perhaps one answer is found at schools already. How do schools get the attention of students now? First, by what is taught and how it is taught in the classroom. Second, by what is rewarded and what is punished. Third, by what is publicized, celebrated, and invested in. Details follow:

WHAT IS TAUGHT AND HOW IT IS TAUGHT

Students spend most of their time at school in classrooms being taught by teachers. What teachers teach and how they teach it will determine, more than any other factors that educators can control, what students learn and how they learn it.

If a school needs to clearly communicate to students that there is a new, grassroots commitment to causing learning, then there is no better place to communicate that, exemplify that, and implement that than in each classroom. What exactly could be done to communicate this commitment to causing learning and to implement this commitment to causing learning so students are fully informed and so students are increasingly supportive of the new commitment as they increasingly benefit from the new commitment through increased learning? Please read the following list, and then add to it:

1. No class time is wasted. Instruction is from bell to bell. If students begin to pack their book with two minutes left in class, they are told to unpack, get back to work, and, as a comparison, they are told that the school basketball team does not leave the gymnasium court until the final second ticks off the clock.
2. Teachers often create designs for and displays in their room. Include posters, made by students, that communicate the idea that the purpose of a school is to cause learning.

3. Some classes begin with a one- or two-minute writing task. On a given day, the opening writing topic could be "why is the purpose of our school to cause learning?"
4. On another day, the opening writing task could be, "You have noticed several changes at school this year. Pick one of those changes and explain what you think the reasons are for that change. Explain also what you think the results from that change will be."
5. "Next week, we will be working on fractions, you already have experience with fractions, like if you are 12-1/2 years old. Your homework for tomorrow is to make a list of ten everyday uses of fractions and to think of one activity we could do in class that would help everyone learn more about fractions."
6. Students always get tests back, homework back, projects back fully graded with meaningful comments within two days of when the work was turned in. How does this cause learning? The assignment is still fresh on the minds of students, so their grade and the teacher's comments become more meaningful because they were prompt. Teachers can stagger due dates so the grading time required fits in the two-day schedule. Tell students that this two-day schedule is part of your commitment to causing learning.
7. Students are always fully informed of what they will be doing in class for the next week. Knowing what is to be learned helps make that learning happen. "Oh, neat, next week we are going to work on the geography of the Pacific Coast states. I've been there. I can bring in lots of pictures and stuff from when we visited there."
8. On every paper, assignment or other handout that teachers give to students, the words "the purpose of school is to cause learning" can be featured. For variety, teachers could include statements or questions such as, "What are you doing right now to cause yourself to learn?" and "Learning is caused. It does not just happen by itself. We make learning happen."
9.

10.

WHAT IS REWARDED AND WHAT IS PUNISHED?

Think about what is rewarded at schools. Does very much come to mind or not? Think about what is punished at school. Is that list longer or not?

Schools punish misbehavior. If rules are broken, if instructions are defied, if the code of conduct for students is violated, there will be punishments.

Students are reminded of what not to do with each punishment they receive or someone else receives.

Do schools reward good behavior? If at all, rewarding good behavior is probably done far less than misbehavior is punished. Is there more good behavior at school than there is misbehavior? Very likely the answer is "yes," as most students do what they are supposed to do most of the time. Could learning about behavior that is right, that is good, that is desired be caused if more effort was made to reward, acknowledge, and appreciate such proper behavior? Yes.

Do schools reward, acknowledge, and appreciate academic achievement by students? One way to confirm that the purpose of a school is to cause learning is to reward students who learn, who learn the most, who work hardest to learn, who improve the most in their efforts to learn. The note a teacher writes on a student's paper, the call or e-mail to a parent or guardian about excellent work their child did in school, the college letter of recommendation a teacher writes for a high school senior, all of these are person-to-person, grassroots ways to reward academic achievement. Please think of additional ways to reward good behavior and excellent learning.

WHAT IS PUBLICIZED, CELEBRATED, AND INVESTED IN

A high school decides to offer a new class in personal finance. This class could cause learning that students use and benefit from for a lifetime. Not much is said about the class. It is listed in the school's curriculum guideline.

The same high school competes in the regional soccer championship game. Signs and posters about the game are seen throughout the school. T-shirts are worn to promote attendance at the game. Public address announcements are made to publicize the game. The school's daily television news program features interviews with coaches, players, and fans. Tickets to the game are sold during lunch at a discount. The school's team wins a very competitive 2–1 match. A celebration is held at the school during lunch the next day.

Soccer is a fascinating sport. Winning the regional championship is a thrilling accomplishment. The excitement surrounding the soccer team is genuine and is part of the high school experience. Yet, mastering personal finance is more important. Long after the students have stopped playing soccer, they will still need to know how to manage money.

The school should celebrate the soccer team's achievement, and the excitement that the publicity about the soccer team generated was worthwhile. Now, use that celebration and publicity as a standard, and ask "Did we do as much to publicize the new personal finance class as we did to publicize the soccer team's regional championship game?"

Students notice what is publicized at school, celebrated at school, and invested in at school. By making sure that learning is publicized, celebrated, and invested in more than anything else at school, a clear message is sent to students—learning is the top priority.

At the grassroots level of each school, the messages sent can be controlled to match the priority that is set. In some ways, those messages establish the priority no matter what the official statement of the school's mission is or what the school's stated purpose is. Since the purpose of a school is to cause learning, the messages sent through what is publicized, celebrated, and invested in need to support the purpose.

LEADERSHIP BY STUDENTS

The very experienced principal of a middle school had been convinced for years that top-down reform of education never worked. Her favorite evidence to support her conclusion was that every top-down reform of education was followed in a few years by another top-down reform of education. No matter what each new reform required, her school complied completely; however, throughout the coming and going of each top-down reform, the principal, faculty, and staff kept their primary efforts directed toward the school's enduring theme: "Learn. Learn more. Keep Learning."

During one faculty meeting, a teacher asked this question: "All of us are dedicated to learning. It's what this school has always been about. We do a good job. I just wish we could get the great students to feel more of a challenge and the average and below average students to feel more of a 'dissatisfaction,' I guess you would call it, with average or below average results. How can we get all of our students to take more responsibility for learning?"

The principal was thinking of an answer when another teacher spoke. "Ask them. If we ask the students, they will tell us what they think. Let's all talk to our first-period class tomorrow and see what they tell us. Just take a few minutes, but ask them to tell us what they think students could do to accept more responsibility for finding academic challenges or for getting below average and average work up to good or great work."

Mrs. Madison was eager to have this discussion with her first period eighth-grade geometry class. The class had done very good work with the complexities of geometry. Some students quickly mastered the concepts and skills. Other students needed more time, guidance, encouragement, and different teaching methods, but Mrs. Madison made sure that everyone learned geometry.

A sign in her room said, "The shortest distance between two points is a straight line. The shortest distance between not knowing and knowing is thinking plus working plus asking questions." The classroom atmosphere was one of thinking, working, and exploring questions. With that atmosphere, the discussion about school would be vibrant and productive.

Mrs. Madison explained the plan for class today, and today's homework was collected. Today's sequence of activities was listed on the board and was discussed briefly. "Before we put the homework problems on the board, we have two questions that every first-period class is discussing today. The principal and the teachers talked about this yesterday at a faculty meeting. We would like your ideas on two topics."

"First, what could students do to accept the responsibility for finding more academic challenges? You know, when something is really easy for you and you could do harder work, what could students themselves do to find that harder, more challenging work? Second, what could students do to go from average or below average work to good or great work? Think of going from C grade or lower to B and A grades."

Hands went up immediately; although, everyone knew there would be five to ten seconds of silent thinking time. Mrs. Madison had disciplined her students to think before speaking. A few more hands were up after the seven seconds of thinking time. The students were eager to be heard on these topics and listened politely to each other's thoughts.

> Student 1: Get rid of cheating, especially people who copy homework. How can that help anybody learn?
>
> Student 2: Give us more time to go to the library and to the computer lab.
>
> Student 3: Do more stuff with computers. We really like computers. And if we have our own smart phone or other technology stuff, let us use that at school. We use it all the time everywhere else.
>
> Student 4: Could we have a class in astronomy? I'm really interested in planets and stars. In science we take about two days on that. It's never enough time. Why can't we have some neat science classes? I went to a science museum last summer. It was so cool. We could make our own science museum or astronomy place.
>
> Student 5: If anyone gets a bad grade, make them do it over to get a better grade. Some teachers allow that. Other teachers never allow it.
>
> Student 6: If you have an A in a class, you should get to do something extra that you really like. I have an A in geometry. I really like camping. Let me do some project on how geometry shows up in camping. Maybe I could design a better tent with geometry.

Student 7: I never do well in science class. I just don't like science. I don't see the point of science. I like my other classes. Astronomy sounds neat. I would do better in astronomy because it would not be the same old science.

Student 8: I play on the football team. We love our tough games. We really want to beat the best teams, so we work harder if a game is against a good team. We goof off if we play an easy team. That's how geometry is for me. It's tough, so I have to work more. The other classes are easy, so I never work as much. I get better grades in geometry even with it being so hard. Maybe the other classes should be more like geometry. I work hard, but it doesn't feel like work because it is interesting when we do a lot of different stuff.

Student 9: Everybody knows who the easy teachers are and who the hard teachers are. Some students do everything to avoid the hard teachers. Tell the easy teachers that students know it will be easy, and get those teachers to change things.

Student 10: We have an honor roll for good grades. Maybe we should have an almost honor roll. People who get close to honor roll but never quite get there, I mean, they might give up trying. Give them a reason to keep trying.

Student 11: All the sports give trophies and things like that. There aren't any trophies in any classes. Why not?

Student 12: A lot of students are lazy. Their bad grades are nothing new. They made bad grades and got in trouble in elementary school. They don't care about better grades. They don't care if they fail. It sounds bad, but it's true. I think they bring it on themselves because they are lazy. Maybe the school could send them somewhere else.

Student 13: My older brother is in college. He says it costs a lot of money, but he got this great scholarship. In high school he made the best grades, and he got college paid for. Maybe some people don't know about stuff like that.

Student 14: I wish I could be in high school now. I'm pretty tired of middle school. Maybe there would be a way to get to high school a year faster.

Student 15: Yes, I agree. Middle school is easy. Just keep up with the work, and don't do stupid things. As for grades, does anybody care about middle school grades? Colleges look at how you did in high school. Nobody checks on how we did in middle school. Maybe we could start earning those credits for high school graduation in eighth grade. Then it would matter.

Mrs. Madison knew that it was time to work on geometry. She also knew that her notes about all of the students' comments would be very interesting to the principal. Some of the ideas from the students could be seriously considered while others would not go anywhere.

Still, the discussion had confirmed that if you ask students for their ideas about school, you will hear quite a range of sincere thoughts. Grassroots school improvement should include input from students and, when possible according to professional judgment and consistency with school purpose, implementation of some student suggestions.

Some adjustments based on the age of students will be needed. Input from elementary school students will be quite different versus input from high school students. The additional years of life experience and of school experience will be among the factors. Still, seeking input from all students can provide a way to build mutual commitment and can provide some ideas that would come from no other source.

School is not the only demand on the time, effort, and talent of students. Students have responsibilities to their families, and families need to spend time together on meaningful family activities. High school students may have part-time jobs. Students may do volunteer work in the community. Students may take dancing lessons or be involved with a church youth group. School deserves a major commitment from each student and each family, yet the students and their families have other important commitments to honor.

School does not have to complete with these other commitments. School can enhance some of those commitments and can build upon some of those commitments. The student who takes dance lessons could work with a teacher to show students how dancing has changed over the decades and centuries. The class could analyze what different dance trends reveal about a changing society. This student who excels in dance now becomes an honorary teacher who helps cause new learning for other students in her class.

The knowledge and skills that students gain from wholesome experiences away from school can be connected to and applied to what needs to be learned at school. That approach would open many resources for grassroots school improvement activities in classrooms where students contribute to the learning experience in very dynamic ways. Can a top-down, political, bureaucratic, mandated education reform do that? What do you, the reader, think?

10

Former Educators

Knowledge, experience, insight, wisdom, understanding, awareness, and skills are among the many resources that former educators can bring to grassroots school improvement efforts. Most former educators may have retired from teaching and/or school administration after a long career. Other former educators left teaching and/or school administration prior to retirement due to personal, family, or career changes or due to staff reductions. Please note the small number of former educators who were removed from school work due to nonperformance problems or noncompliance issues is not the topic of this chapter.

"We congratulate Mr. Clay for his thirty-five years of teaching and of school administration. He taught middle school for eight years, then taught high school for seven years, then was a high school assistant principal for five years, and was a high school principal for fifteen years. He has been devoted to students and to his colleagues. He always went the extra mile for everyone."

"In retirement, he plans to be a very involved grandfather, a good golfer, a church volunteer, and an occasional substitute teacher. We wish him the best, and we are glad that he will be back in schools for some time to come. Mr. Clay, we hope you will share some thoughts with us."

Mr. Clay smiled as a few tears began to fill his eyes. The faculty of his high school stood to applaud and to express very sincere appreciation to a superior educator, a true friend, and an exemplary leader.

"Thank you for your very kind words and actions today. It has been an honor to work with you at this outstanding school. My retirement plans are simple. I will volunteer more at my church. I will babysit often with my grandchildren. My wife and I will travel. And, I will do some substitute teaching. Teaching was my first love in this profession. It will be good to be back in the classroom. So if you need a good substitute, ask for me when you phone in your absence."

"One other thought along those lines. After you have worked in education as long as I have, you begin to realize that what we do each day in our work with students is what does the most good. How many times have we seen politicians and bureaucrats tell us what's wrong with schools and what needs to be done to fix schools? Too many. How many times have you seen those politicians and bureaucrats actually come to school and do this work or, at least, talk to us? Just about never. That will probably never change."

"What you do every day for students and with students is what matters most in education. Great teaching has always worked. Great teaching will always work. You are great teachers, great counselors, great staff members, and it has been my honor to work with you."

There was only one other retirement at the high school this year. That is unusual, but the way the finances of retirement programs were changing, many people had to decide to work several more years than they had planned. Mrs. Consuelo Fatima was a legendary teacher of Latin and Spanish. She began teaching at age twenty-two and taught for six years. She then stayed at home with her twin daughters until they began school. Mrs. Fatima returned to teach for the next twenty-eight years.

Whether a high school student spent one year with Mrs. Fatima or four years, the language being studied was learned thoroughly. After some very thoughtful comments were made by a former student of Mrs. Fatima's—this former student is also a Spanish teacher at the same high school—Consuelo Fatima spoke to her colleagues.

"Thank you. *Muchas gracias.* Thank you very much. I have loved my many years at this school. I have been here for twenty-eight years, and I have taught for thirty-four years total. It is a blessing to be able to retire, but I will stay very busy. My husband owns a restaurant. I am going to teach cooking lessons there as we expand the business to have culinary classes."

"I also plan to be a volunteer here. I want to come teach your classes for you so you can go watch each other teach. We never get to learn from each other. I will volunteer to teach your classes so you can go learn what other teachers are doing and so you can see what your students are doing in other classes. So, I'll be back. I could never leave teaching forever."

Mr. Clay and Mrs. Fatima spoke after this faculty meeting where their retirements had been celebrated. They talked about how intrigued they were with the possibilities of what they could do for students, for teachers, for education from the position of former full-time educators to retired part-time educators.

Mr. Clay knew of five other administrators who were retiring at the same time he was. Those five colleagues joined Mr. Clay to discuss retirement plans and how continued work in schools could fit into those plans. The six retirees knew each other well from years of administrative meetings and from years of trading ideas. Part of their conversation is below.

Mr. Clay: It is great to see everyone. These are unusual days as we conclude our long careers in education. All of us have plans for the retirement years, and it has been really interesting to hear about the trips everyone plans to take and the hobbies we will enjoy. It sounds as if all of us will be spending lots of time with our grandchildren. One reason to meet today was to enjoy each other's company one more time before we retire. Another reason is to consider ways that we could still be of service to schools. Among the six of us, we have about two hundred years total experience in teaching and in school administration. I just hope we can put all of our knowledge and experience to good use in ways that will continue to help schools.

I intend to substitute teach one or two days each week. I loved being a teacher. When I'm in a school, I'll offer to help in any way I am needed in addition to the substitute teacher work. I just see retired educators as an untapped resource for schools. What do you think?

Administrator 1: Give me a year to relax first. I've been at this for thirty-five years. It's all I've ever done. I might try something completely different. I might play a lot of golf. Of course, we know more about education than most people, but we also deserve a break from the action. That's one reason we decided to retire.

I still like this work, but at age fifty-seven, I think there is time to try something new. So maybe in a year I'll be relaxed enough and ready to help with schools unless I find something else that takes my time and becomes a real second career.

Administrator 2: I wonder if we could do something electronically. Maybe we could become the founders of an advice website. Teachers and principals and other people who work at schools could e-mail us asking for advice. We could post lots of information and ideas on the website. There would be links for teachers to share great lesson plans and for school counselors to share good resources. We could get permission to post articles about education.

I've always thought that graduate schools where our teachers go to earn degrees should share the research papers that graduate students write if the students agreed. This website could do that too. There would be a lot of rules to follow about confidentiality or copyrights, but one of the school district's technology experts is retiring. I bet she could help get this idea going.

Administrator 3: I wonder if I should just get out of the way of the next generation of teachers and school administrators and everyone else. I went to college forty-five years ago after I was in the army for five years. I worked in schools for forty years. I'm sixty-eight years old, and I feel it. I'm pretty old-fashioned. I think books are better than any technology gadget. I think spelling counts. I think people expect schools to solve every problem in society that every child or teenager has.

Times have changed, I guess, but students need to dress correctly, behave correctly, work harder, and not have excuses made for them. I'm not just going to sit around in retirement, but I'm not so sure that my experience and my judgment are what the new teachers and principals are looking for. And don't get me started on the politicians. Will they ever realize how little they know about education and how much confusion they cause with the unnecessary laws they pass about schools? Maybe I should run for the state legislature and go tell those people what they don't know about schools.

Administrator 4: Count me in with anything I can do to help schools. We are allowed to retire after thirty years of school work, and that's what I'm doing, but at age fifty-two, I've got another fifteen or twenty years of good work left in me. I've thought about substitute teaching. I'm certified to be a guidance counselor, and maybe I could do that part-time. I think the retirement system allows that. I would keep working except what I would get paid to work is not enough more than what I'll get paid in retirement to be worth it.

Administrator 5: I worked in banking for eight years before I became a teacher. I had my teaching certification from my college classes. I studied business, finance, and banking. The bank I worked for got bought, and the new owner dismissed a lot of workers, including me. So, I started teaching and then became an assistant principal.

Thirty-three years in education means I can retire fairly comfortably financially, but I know I'll be looking for things to do. I don't see myself substitute teaching day to day, but a long-term substitute teaching schedule could work. If a teacher is out for maternity leave, I could take her place. That way I get to work with the same students each day.

I really like the technology idea. It would be like a telephone helpline, only it's on the Internet. Teachers and principals get so busy that they rarely talk to each other about good ideas or how to handle situations. Doing that online could be really helpful.

Mr. Clay: It is so good to hear everyone's plans and ideas. This is June. School is out. All of us will finish our work this month. I'd like to meet one more time this month, and let's have someone from Human Resources meet with us so we can get that advice on what we can do as retirees. Let's have that technology expert who is retiring join us and see how to set up our helpline website; maybe it's an online help website. I'll e-mail everyone with an update, but since Friday morning worked this week, is Friday morning at 9:00 next week good for everyone? Yes? Great. Let's plan on that.

Life circumstances, family obligations, health factors, and other opportunities will impact how much former educators will be involved with schools.

That is also true for parents, guardians, community members, and other individuals or groups. Grassroots efforts do not need full-time participation by every possible participant; rather, there is some contribution that each person can make. The sum of those contributions can truly improve schools.

Mr. Clay was pleased that every person who attended the first meeting returned for the follow-up meeting. The Human Resources manager and the technology expert joined the six retiring administrators. During the follow-up meeting, the administrators who were interested in becoming substitute teachers were shown how to complete the online application for that. The idea- and advice-sharing website concept got a lot of attention. A schedule was agreed to for setting up a prototype of the website and starting some tests and trials to see how it works.

There was one surprise idea. Some retired educators have hobbies they have overlooked but now have time for. From golf to knitting, from travel to pottery, from cooking to carpentry, these hobbies could have an academic side. It was suggested that the new idea-sharing and advice-giving website could include a "speakers' bureau" listing of retired educators and the topics they could make classroom presentations about. Teachers could invite retirees to be guest speakers.

One elementary school principal heard about this resource and saw it as the solution to a community day activity she had dreamed of. The plan was to have thirty or forty presentations in the school at one time. Students would sign up for the two presentations they were most interested in. Retired educators, parents, guardians, community members could come to school and make two consecutive presentations. A teacher would be in each presentation to help make connections between the school curriculum and the topic of the presentations.

The community day became so successful that other local elementary schools and middle schools borrowed the idea. Local media coverage of community days was very positive. Learning was caused through an idea that began as part of a discussion of retiring and soon-to-be-former educators. Although, as Mr. Clay realized, former is misleading. Former full-time, perhaps, but never completely former. Retirement did not change the heart, mind, and soul of forever educator, Mr. Clay.

Mr. Clay's substitute teaching was filled with the joys and frustrations, the accomplishments and the disappointments that occur in the classroom. During the substitute teaching assignment he accepted, a teacher had to be away from school for three weeks to have surgery and to recover from surgery. Mr. Clay liked the continuity of work with the same classes for an extended time. He was rather weary after those three weeks and was reminded of how physically demanding it is to teach well.

Mr. Clay also felt some fatigue in terms of heart and soul, not because he was discouraged but because he saw the continuation of a trend that needed attention. In the six high school classes that Mr. Clay taught during those three weeks, 11 of his 152 students had a grandparent or grandparents as guardians. These 11 students seemed to be doing well at school, but in conversations Mr. Clay had with two grandparents when he called them to report great work done in class by their grandchildren, he heard those dear people talk about how different it was to rear grandchildren from how it had been to rear their own children.

Mr. Clay talked to some school counselors and a school social worker to see if any support was being provided to grandparents who found themselves back in the role of parent, but this time with two generations between the adult and the child. The people Mr. Clay talked to knew of no such support program, but they confirmed that while the numbers were not large, the number of students being reared by a grandparent was increasing every year.

Mr. Clay decided to create a support group, which he called Grand Ideas for Grandparents. The goal of the group would be to give grandparents who were rearing their grandchildren a source of ideas, guidance, answers, and help. It would give them a way to talk with other grandparents who were rearing grandchildren.

Grand Ideas for Grandparents worked quite well. It was not complicated or complex. It had no expenses. It just responded to a need by providing direct person-to-person time, help, encouragement, and resources. No new laws, regulations, policies, or taxes were needed to create or to continue this support group. The energy of one former educator and the help of many current educators, especially school counselors made this happen. School improvement of, by, and for the grass roots could claim another victory.

"I am a candidate for our state senate. This is my first campaign for public office. My career was in education. I have forty years of experience as a teacher and as a school administrator. I know that there are many issues on the minds of voters—jobs, taxes, the quality of our roads, public safety, health care, and much more. I have concerns about those issues also. The truth is that about half of the state government's budget goes to education, so I bring forty years of experience and knowledge to the biggest expenditure of state government."

"I will provide details of my position on all major issues, but today I will emphasize education. I will oppose the current proposal for yet another major reform of education. In my forty years as an educator, I saw a new reform every five to ten years. They never worked very well. Some did not work at all. Few did much good. Some did harm."

"Instead of more micromanagement from the state government, I would suggest that the state government establish goals and let each school district work with each local school to figure out how to reach those goals in each classroom. Now, I will be glad to answer any questions you have."

The reporters had several questions, and the candidate had a clear answer for each, as shown below. Note that the answers may not have been perfectly politically correct, but this sixty-eight-year-old candidate had already decided that his campaign would be unlike many modern campaigns. He had decided to bluntly tell the facts and to frankly tell his ideas. The voters could decide whether blunt and frank were appealing.

> Reporter 1: Your campaign material says you will be blunt and frank. The political process relies on compromise. Can you work in a system that is full of compromises?
>
> Candidate: I can work in that system, but I don't expect to compromise very much. Here's why. Compromise is practical, but what it ends up with may not be a real solution to a problem. One group wants the state to require more testing in schools. Another group wants less testing. Compromise says just keep it like it is, a medium amount of testing, but is medium the right amount or just the politically practical amount? Instead of making schools do what the political process can get approved, it's better for schools to do what is best for students. No national or state political process that lives on compromise can create superior schools because compromise seeks an action that gets votes, not necessarily the best action that gets the best results.
>
> Reporter 2: State government never has enough money for all of its increasing obligations. Colleges, schools, roads, state parks, health programs are always in search of more money from state government. What would you do to deal with financial limits that always face state government?
>
> Candidate: Not every problem is solved with more money being spent by the government. If there is a way to solve a problem, that is the concern of and under the jurisdiction of state government. Let's look at all of the possible solutions, including some that cost no money. About twenty years ago, this state had a big education reform law. Taxes went up to pay for all of the changes. Now, most of that law is gone, changed, done away with because politicians changed their minds. But the taxes that went up to pay for that law never went away or never were reduced. The law is gone, for the most part, but the taxes are still here completely.
>
> Reporter 3: Can you give us an example of a way to reform education without spending more tax money?
>
> Candidate: Yes, I can. First, beware of the word "reform." Education does not need to be reformed. The form we have now is fine. We just need better results. Now, here's the idea you asked for. There are hundreds and thousands of retired educators in this state. Many of them were excellent teachers or principals or

guidance counselors. They know a lot about schools. They know a lot about how to help students learn.

So, let's recruit the very capable former educators who would like to make a real contribution to school again. Let's get the great former educators to mentor college students who are studying to become teachers. Let's have the great former teachers work with student teachers and with first-year teachers. We could have some great former teachers work with current teachers who, for whatever reason, are at a point in their career where they need some guidance or direction or other help.

There's more. Let's get some former principals who were really good school leaders and managers to work with first-year principals. Former counselors could work with first-year counselors.

That's not all. Let's get some former elementary school, middle school, and high school teachers to work with college professors of education. Many of those college professors have been away from elementary schools, middle schools, or high schools for a long time. They need to hear from people who spent a career in those schools.

Why not let former teachers be a resource to college professors? Former principals could help graduate school professors prepare the next generation of school administrators.

That is a much longer answer than you expected, but I've done this work forever, and I think about schools all the time. We don't need to reform schools. We just need to get more creative in our solutions, and whenever possible, we need to keep government from making work at school more complex and bureaucratic instead of more human, personal, and productive.

Reporter 4: Are there issues other than education that you think state government could find creative solutions to without spending more money?

Candidate: My experience is education. I can tell you more about schools than you knew existed. Other people are experts in other areas. I would listen to their expertise and offer a few questions or ideas. Maybe the state government needs an electronic suggestion box so government employees and residents of the state could offer ideas.

I'm sure there are times when only more money can deal with some costly and complicated problems, but my first approach would be to look for innovative solutions that use thinking instead of money whenever that can do the job.

Reporter 5: One more question, please. The governor has proposed a major reform of education. Another candidate for governor has proposed a completely different reform of education. What guidance would you give the voters as they evaluate these reform plans?

Candidate: You can predict my answer to that. First, ask those politicians how many years they have worked in a school. The answer is zero. Be very concerned at that point. Second, ask them where they got their ideas about education? Did they listen to current educators and to former educators? Did they listen to their campaign consultants? Did they simply borrow trendy ideas from other states? Third, challenge them to go spend time in schools before they recommend a reform. Challenge them to withdraw their reform plans, which will not work, and go listen to people across this state to find out what is working well in our state.

We have many great teachers, great schools, great principals, and great students. Let's find out what is working and expand that instead of having one more expensive and temporary reform of education that will not work.

Now, you have news stories to prepare, and I have some campaigning to do. Thank you for being here today. By the way, I doubt that many of you who work in journalism write or do many stories about education. I read the newspaper, and I see the news on television. There is very little coverage of education.

I would encourage you to go talk to people who work in schools. Talk to people who used to work in schools. Find out what they know and what they suggest. Make that information a big story or a series of stories. Maybe the people who want to be governor will notice your stories and get the idea that listening to people is a better start for improving schools than their massive reform plans could ever be.

THE FORMER EDUCATOR RETURNS

"I have been asked to speak to our retired teachers group today because of experiences I have had during my retirement years. Some of you may be interested in doing what I have found to be very rewarding. Some of you may have other obligations or interests or hobbies that take all of your time. I do hope that you will find what I have to tell you to be interesting."

"During my first year of retirement, there were several promises I had made to myself that I was determine to keep. I had always wanted to see Europe, so my husband and I took the trip of a lifetime to London, Amsterdam, Rome, Florence, Paris, and some lovely villages we had never heard of, but the touring company knew all about. It was the perfect trip."

"My husband is quite the golfer, so I took golf lessons, and I'm not bad at that game. He has a group of friends who play together once or twice a week. The wives of that group have started playing together once a week. We hope to teach our grandchildren how to play golf next summer."

"Well, travel and golf are both good activities, but I was used to teaching for thirty-four years, and, as you know, teaching is nonstop activity. Even in retirement, I was soon looking for more to do than travel and golf. I found what I was looking for, or better yet, it found me."

"At the golf course one day, I met two university professors. They work with undergraduates and with graduate students in the college of education.

They said one student was doing research that involved interviews with former teachers. Could the student talk with me, they asked. I was glad to be of help. Well, the discussion was just fascinating. The graduate student's research area dealt with what keeps teachers on the job for a teaching career of thirty years or longer despite the many difficulties and heartbreaks."

"After that interview, I started thinking about the young teachers I had known during my career who left teaching after only a few years. I always wondered if it was because of a better job offer, family matters, if they just realized that they were not cut out for teaching, or if nobody helped them through the first few years of teaching when it really can be overwhelming."

"So I thought, I could help new teachers. I have the experience, the knowledge, and now I have the time. I worked it out with a principal I had known for years, and she worked it out with the school district. As a volunteer, I would come to school one day each week and spend the day with a first-year or second-year teacher who wanted a mentor. I would observe classes, look at recent and upcoming lesson plans, take a lot of notes, and then talk with the teacher during planning period, at lunch, or after school."

"It has been wonderful. I really think that one first-year teacher I worked with is twice the teacher she would have been without the mentoring. She told me that our discussions and my advice to her changed everything. How about that? Nothing all that special, just taking what my decades in the classroom revealed to me and giving that insight to a new teacher, plus answering her questions, making suggestions, pointing out what she did well, and guiding her to realize what she could do better."

"I love my time at school with these new teachers. Here's something I did not expect. One experienced teacher with twelve years of teaching so far asked me to spend a day with him. He had heard about the work I was doing with some new teachers at his school. Now this twelve-year veteran of teaching is an outstanding teacher, but he is eager to improve. He is at a point in his career when he does not want to get stale, or in a rut, or even lazy."

"He is much better than he gives himself credit for. We had great conversations. I was very Socratic with him, and he usually ended up answering his own questions as I led him through some thinking that perhaps comes only with the second or third decade of teaching."

"So, I am here today to let you know that schools still need you, and if you like to be needed, then we can find schools where you can be the person who makes a big difference in the career achievements of a new teacher. It really is similar to what we did with our students. We made sure they learned the subject we taught. This time, we make sure that new teachers learn about school as a workplace, learn about how to manage their time, learn how to communicate with parents, learn how to implement a discipline system, learn how to stay healthy and take good care of themselves."

"So, please, when our meeting today is over, let's talk if you are interested. I have a list of principals and of school district officials who you can contact to begin the process of becoming a mentor to a teacher."

"I'm still going to travel. I'm still going to play golf. But I am also still going to help improve schools. Oh, yeah, this is volunteer work. It is not extra income. It sure is good for the heart and soul, so that is a different type of income. You will go through a short training program that I will teach. You will be screened as a school district volunteer. You will give the principal a report using a very simple form for each day you spend at school."

"We are looking into a license you could get as a teacher mentor, so that may come. The requirements are a college degree, a graduate school degree, at least twenty years of teaching and/or school administration, and the training program I provide."

"I encourage you to give this idea very thorough consideration. I love my retirement. I love it even more because of this teacher mentor program. Golf once a week is plenty for me. A trip every six months is plenty. Being needed at school and making a difference at school, it means a lot to know that I can still do that. If that would mean a lot to you, let's talk today. If you would like to set up a golf game with me, we can do that also but after I meet with everyone who would like to become a teacher mentor."

"Thanks for this opportunity to speak to our group today. It is always so good to see all of you. Now, you get to hear from another member of our retired teachers club whose presentation is called 'My Reading Coach Is Here!'"

"Thank you. My presentation will be short because what I am going to say we all have experienced. I taught elementary school for twenty-eight years. I always put a large emphasis on reading in my classroom. I taught third or fourth grade usually, so the students brought reading skills with them, but some students brought serious reading problems with them. I knew I could help each student master reading if I could spend time one-to-one with each struggling reader. How could I just concentrate for an hour on one student when I had a classroom of twenty-four students?"

"In my last year of teaching, I promised myself that I would volunteer to come back to school one day every week or two and work individually with any student who needed extra help with reading. The principal loved the idea, and she made all of the necessary arrangements to take care of legal requirements and policy issues related to volunteers."

"So, in January of the first school year I was retired, I began doing my reading coach volunteer work. It is a joy. The reading gains these students make is uplifting. All they needed was some individual guidance. The teachers love it when I visit because they know that the students who need a lot of individual attention will get it while the teacher can keep working with the rest of the class."

"Just last week, I walked into the classroom, and a nine-year-old third-grader saw me, smiled, and told everyone, 'My reading coach is here!' We read together for the next hour. She has made so much progress that she may not need a reading coach much longer, but there will be other students who need my help."

"So if working one-to-one with a student whose reading skills will improve with your help appeals to you, let's talk after this meeting. Now you have two ways to apply your experience. You can mentor a new teacher, or you can coach a new reader. Either way, you can really make a difference."

"I am increasingly convinced that person-to-person activity like these opportunities provide are among the best ways to improve schools. Former teachers know so much and can offer so much. The more we can help schools, the better the school results will be, plus I would rather donate my time to help schools than see taxes go up to pay for some school reform plan or similar initiative."

"So, I hope some of you will join me. Then someday soon you will have the thrill of hearing a nine-year-old say joyously 'My reading coach is here!' when you walk in the classroom."

The insights, knowledge, experiences, lessons learned, successes created, problems solved, and understanding gained throughout a long career in education go with an educator when he or she retires or changes professions. Some former educators may find it very appealing and very rewarding to make new contributions to schools.

These skilled, experienced, insightful people can be part of grassroots efforts that improve schools. They can also be part of efforts that seek to sufficiently inform political leaders of school reality so those political leaders will realize that top-down education reform does not work.

We now turn to current educators and the virtually endless ways that they can cause learning in the minds of students plus the many ways they can improve schools through grassroots work.

11

Current Educators

Of all possible grassroots endeavors to improve schools, nothing is more potent, effective, productive, powerful, and important than the work which effective teachers do in classrooms to cause learning.

For people who continue to call for education reform, it can be honestly said to those reform advocates that effective teachers are the ultimate reform of and reformers of education.

Teachers—you are the reform. You are the reformers. You are the revolution. You are the revolutionaries. You are the radicals as the ancient heritage of that word expresses—"radical" meaning "root," which says that teachers are the fundamental, essential, support structure of schools being places where learning is caused.

What you do with students is the most significant factor of all factors that educators can control. No top-down reform of education can match the face-to-face, brain-to-brain, mind-to-mind, person-to-person, teacher-to-student impact that you can have.

Teachers can be the ultimate reform of and the ultimate reformers of education. High-quality, high-impact, dedicated, determined, competent, caring, effective teachers are more favorably impactful for education in general, for students collectively, for students individually than any top-down political reform of education can be.

Teachers cannot have that impact with an attitude that communicates "There are only sixteen days to go in the school year," or "I'm not sick, but I'm calling in sick this Friday. I know I did that last Friday, but that's just the way it is." Or, "Let's watch a video today. I have computer work to do, so be quiet, pay attention, watch the video, and take some notes."

When the desired results occur in classrooms, the advocates of top-down political reform of education have less support for their mandates. That suggests that the strongest antidote to top-down, political, bureaucratic, systemic reform of education is effective grassroots work at the essential grassroots level—the classroom.

Political reforms of education imply that education can be manufactured and that learning can be manufactured. If the newest political reform can finally arrange the mechanics and the logistics of education correctly, the desired results will follow. Not a chance. Education is not manufactured. Learning is not manufactured. Learning is caused through purposeful work done with the leadership and management of highly effective and highly impactful teachers.

Of course, for schools to maximize results, there must be highly effective and highly impactful principals, assistant principals, school counselors, and staff members. Still, students spend most of their time at school in classrooms with teachers. That is where education happens. That is where school improvement happens.

For some people who would seek to reform education, school is a spectator activity. Those people may be at a think tank writing position papers about schools, or they may be a candidate for public office giving a speech about schools. While think-tankers write and candidates talk, teachers are in classrooms doing the ultimate grassroots work in the crusade to improve schools.

Education happens in classrooms. Top-down education reform plans happen elsewhere and then are imposed on schools. Evaluate the logic or the missing logic of top-down education reform.

A word of very practical reality: even when great teachers get great results, there can continue to be appeals from some think tanks, politicians, editorial writers, foundations, or advocacy groups for top-down reform of education. Why? Think tanks are in business to present points of view rather than to tell great teachers that they are doing great work. Politicians, editorial writers, foundations, and advocacy groups have their agendas and motives.

In the arena of public schools, those voices deserve to be heard. Respond to those voices with the confidence of an intellectual democracy participant. Make your voice heard, and use your intellect to show quantitatively and qualitatively that what you are doing in your classroom with your students is working; therefore, top-down reforms of education need not invade here or interfere here.

Each top-down reform is temporary. Great teaching is forever, its impact lasts forever, and it is always effective. Top-down reform tends to be superficial. Great teaching touches the mind and the heart. Current educators can have more positive impact on what is accomplished at schools than any or all top-down, political, bureaucratic, systemic education reforms can have.

Educators are face-to-face with students in classrooms where learning is caused. Top-down political reform originates from miles away and is imposed from miles away. That distance changes the perception of what is needed and of what works. The further you move from the classroom reality, the further you distance yourself from what is needed and from what works.

So, if the classroom is the place where learning happens and if current educators are the people who make that learning happen, why is there continued criticism of and dissatisfaction with schools? We know what works to cause learning in classrooms, so why is maximum learning not yet occurring for every student in every classroom?

A long list of reasons could be provided, but consider a different perspective. There are many classrooms where every student is learning. There are many schools that are getting great results. What is happening in these successful classrooms and schools that could be applied, with modifications as needed, elsewhere? One of the most productive and efficient ways to improve schools that current educators could do is to share with each other the answers to those questions: what works in your classroom, and what works in your school?

Teachers can post their best lesson plans on the school's website. Other teachers can find ideas from those posted lesson plans that could be adapted to their classes. Teachers can post innovative projects they are having students do so other teachers can apply those project ideas as well. Teachers can explain their classroom discipline system, their homework system, their grading method, and their types of quizzes and tests so every teacher becomes aware of the best ideas, methods, and activities.

Teachers throughout a school district or a state could expand the idea-sharing network through electronic media. Using an idea from another teacher does not do the teaching for a teacher. The work of teaching must still be done. When one doctor uses an idea for a surgical procedure that he was told about by another doctor, the newly informed doctor still has to perform the surgery. The point is not that getting good ideas makes anyone's job easier; rather, it makes the results for everyone better.

THE TEACHER, THE PRINCIPAL, AND THE LEGISLATORS

The state's House of Representatives Education Committee was scheduled to hold hearings on several topics including: (1) a set of revisions to the curriculum for each grade in the kindergarten through high school sequence, (2) new requirements for required professional development training for all teachers, and (3) a plan for students to take a state-required test once every two months for half of a school day instead of once a year in April or May for several school days. One state representative had invited an award-winning high school teacher and a highly respected middle school principal, both from the district she represents, to address the Education Committee, to answer questions from committee members, to offer ideas, and to ask questions. The committee chairman opened the meeting with words of introduction for the topic and for the guests.

> Chairman: We welcome all committee members, guests who will testify at this hearing, and audience members whose interest we appreciate. We will begin today by hearing from Ms. Julie Lauren, a very respected teacher of high school chemistry. We will also hear from Mr. Brian Roberts, a very respected middle school principal. Ms. Lauren and Mr. Roberts, please begin with your thoughts on education in general.
>
> Ms. Lauren: During my twenty-two years of teaching middle school science and then of teaching high school chemistry, I have had many wonderful experiences. Some of my students have become teachers. Some have earned graduate degrees in science or in medicine. Of my students, 99 percent passed the science or chemistry class they took with me. Of my students, 61 percent have earned a grade of A or B in my class. That is not due to grade inflation. We do not increase the grade. We increase the work, and we increase the learning, then the grade follows.
>
> I use very many different teaching methods and activities. I do not repeat the same lessons every year. No two students are identical. No two classes of students are identical. I find out what works with each student and with each class. I do not force them into a prepackaged mold. I do insist that the students work and learn, but how we work and how we learn will vary according to what gets the best results on any given day. That is one reason I resist and I oppose generic, cookie-cutter reforms of education that try to impose the exact same tasks and methods and activities and procedures on every teacher and every student. Teaching is a very interactive, unfolding, human process. Schools are not assembly lines.
>
> Mr. Roberts: Years ago, Ms. Lauren and I taught at the same middle school. She was in her third year of teaching when I was in my first year of teaching. I was having a lot of difficulty with teaching. The principal arranged to have a substitute teacher come for me one day so I could spend that day in Ms. Lauren's classroom learning from her and with her.
>
> Everything changed for me from that time on. I was not a superstar teacher overnight, but I was better soon, and I kept improving. I would visit Ms. Lauren's classroom occasionally during my planning period. I would get copies of the materials she prepared for her classes. I did not just duplicate her methods or copy her materials and imitate her in my classroom. I made some adjustments based on what I knew about my students.

As a principal, I insist that the teachers in our school visit other classrooms. I make myself available to teach one class each day so the teacher can observe a colleague and then tell me what was learned. I give them my insights about their classes I taught. At my school, everyone of any age keeps learning. On every measurement of schools used by the state or our school district, the school where I work always surpasses our goals and ranks very high. We trade good ideas, we share success stories, and we work together.

Committee member 1: One of our topics today is a set of drastic changes in the curriculum for kindergarten through high school. The intent of this seems to be that every student will move at the same pace. For example, any student in the state who is taking eighth-grade United States history would have studied the Declaration of Independence, the Revolutionary War, and the Articles of Confederation during weeks six to eight of the school year.

I am told this is to be sure that the curriculum is completed on time each year in each school and to help students who move from one school to another school so they can stay on track. What do you think of these curriculum changes and the schedules that go with them?

Ms. Lauren: I understand the intent, but I am concerned with the assembly line mentality that says every class can or should move at exactly the same pace during the school year. If a student visited a Civil War battlefield during summer vacation and has a great presentation to make about that, let's allow the time.

Whoever created the micromanaged day-to-day and week-to-week curriculum calendar works in some office where there are no students. As far as the curriculum content itself, from what I can tell, each subject at each grade level is supposed to do more than before. That will not be easy, but it can be done if we are given flexibility in the schedule throughout the year. Don't give us more to do and then tell us the exact timing day-to-day for when it is supposed to be done. Each teacher can find a way. We can share our ideas with each other in our schools and in our school districts.

And if there is another big curriculum change some time in the future, involve a lot of current educators in the process of creating the new curriculum. Don't just hire some expensive national consultants and accept their costly concepts as the best. I'll be glad to give you better ideas at no cost and so will many other teachers.

Mr. Roberts: If the new curriculum content and schedule are enacted into state law, we will implement the law. That is our professional obligation. I do have some awareness of the background on these curriculum changes. Several other states have done this, and our state's political leaders and education leaders apparently heard about it at several national conferences of governors or legislators or education officials.

I would ask that you not take action on this now. Post all of the details of the curriculum changes on the state government's website, and e-mail every teacher and school administrator information about these proposed changes. Notify your constituents. Get input from people in our state about these proposals. Then make your decision. Better to make a good decision one year from now than a bad decision now just to beat a certain deadline.

Committee member 2: Our state requires every teacher to get twenty-four hours of professional development credit every year. This committee is considering a plan to increase that to thirty hours next year and thirty-six hours the year after that. Our thought is that there is so much that teachers need to be updated on or trained in that more time is needed. What do you think?

Ms. Lauren: Thirty-six hours of great professional development training could be helpful, but if you ask teachers about most professional development we have to attend, it is just awful. The state and the school districts decide what eighteen of those twenty-four hours will be about. We have to watch some video or take some online quiz or hear some presentation about generic topics or trendy issues that really do not relate to what we do or need to do or need to know.

Before any work is done or money is spent on more professional development expansion, please evaluate what is being done now. It's not just the number of hours, it's also the quality of the program we attend.

Mr. Roberts: The best professional development, according to the teachers at my school, is always during the six hours we get to control. We use that time for our teachers to present their best lessons and teaching ideas to our teachers. It's practical. It involves no money for speakers to come in. It is followed up the rest of the year as people try each other's ideas and keep sharing.

I agree that, before you expand professional development to thirty hours or thirty-six hours, which the state would probably fill with more mandates of generic training that every teacher must go through, find out how much good the current professional development system is doing.

Committee member 3: The topic of testing gets a lot of attention. Our state has a testing schedule that offers options, but most schools end up using three, four, or five school days in April or May to administer the annual tests that the state requires. Some schools use parts of five days. Other schools use all of three days. It varies. One idea has been to have testing for part of one school day every two months instead of having all testing done during one week in the spring. What do you think?

Ms. Lauren: The school year begins in August. If we have a state-required test in October, the students have had only two months of instruction. Maybe that is why some people support the strict curriculum schedule that shows what must be taught each week of the year. Then the October test would measure what was on the curriculum schedule during August and September.

The truth is that people have less confidence in these tests every year. The state keeps changing the test format or the test vendor or the scoring system for the tests. I think there are bigger issues with these tests than the schedule of when we take them.

Mr. Roberts: The teachers at my school send me a copy of every test they give to their students. I read those tests. It helps me keep up with what occurs day-to-day in classrooms. I take those most recent tests with me when I visit classrooms so I can ask students some questions before class. Our teachers create excellent tests, which challenge our students and which truly measure what they have learned.

I have not been convinced that the annual tests we spend a week on each April or May are worth the time and the expense. I would encourage you to keep the testing in the spring, as late in the school year as possible. I would ask that we streamline the tests. Let's find a system that can be completed in two days so we can avoid dedicating a full week to testing every year.

Chairman: Thank you for being with us today. We appreciate the outstanding work you are doing. We also appreciate the important ideas you expressed to us today. Please keep in touch with us, and encourage your colleagues to send us their ideas.

Current educators can be heard by school board members, state legislators, governors, members of Congress, and the president. At a school board meeting, the communication can be face-to-face. Old-fashioned letters can be mailed. E-mails can be sent. Meetings can be attended.

Current educators can be the voice of school reality so people in positions of power and authority can be informed of and, perhaps, persuaded of what is needed in schools and of what is not needed in schools, of what works in schools and what does not work in schools, as those topics are uniquely understood by current educators.

Teachers, school counselors, assistant principals, principals, and staff members can confirm that schools are active, energetic, busy places. Amid all of this activity at schools, many decisions are made every day. Teachers make decisions about lessons, homework, rewards, projects, quizzes, tests, discipline actions, comments to make to students or colleagues, and comments to not make to anyone.

Principals and assistant principals make decisions throughout every school day. Will a request by a teacher for a field trip be approved? Will a request by an athletic team for a fundraiser be approved? Will a request for a high school to host a blood drive be approved? How long will two students who fought be suspended from school? Should criminal charges be filed against a student who stole a laptop computer belonging to the school? Will a teacher who has asked to teach a different grade level next year be told "yes" or "no"? Will a request for a new science class to be added to the curriculum be approved? Will a school group that would like to sponsor a talent show during the school day that students buy a ticket for and miss class to attend be told "yes" or "no"? Will a community group that would like to sponsor a school assembly on Constitution Day be told "yes" or "no"?

How are these decisions and many more school decisions best made? Of course, laws, regulations, and policies must be obeyed. If the school has a policy against fundraising events that take students out of class, the answer to that request is no. In fact, if everyone at the school knows the policy, the request should never be made.

In the absence of a specific policy allowing, requiring, or prohibiting something, judgment must be used. What can guide judgmental decisions so the best decision is made? A clear statement of school purpose. Decisions are then made that are consistent with and supportive of the school purpose.

If a school's purpose statement says, "The purpose of our school is to cause learning," then decisions are made so the most learning and the best learning will occur at school and through the school experience. The group that would like to hold a fundraiser can do that after school ends for the day. Students who would have missed class to attend that fundraising event cannot attend a make-up class after school dismisses for the day.

Current educators can help improve their school at the grassroots level, which is the classroom in particular and the school in its entirety, by making sure that all decisions at the school are consistent with and supportive of the school's purpose. When every decision at a school and every action at a school are consistent with and supportive of the school purpose of causing learning, more learning and better learning will be experienced by more students. A relentless compliance with the school purpose can help get the results that make top-down education reform unnecessary and that show the superiority of improving schools of, by, and for the grassroots level.

When commitment to and abidance by the school purpose permeates a school—every decision made and every action taken are done to cause learning—the desired results are obtained. This is done at the grassroots level. This is done to improve schools and to simultaneously improve the learning experience of students and to enhance the career experience of educators.

The purpose of a school is to cause learning. The purpose of top-down, political, bureaucratic, systemic reform of education may include references to learning, but this reform is filled with a multitude of other purposes, some acknowledged openly and others not mentioned openly.

THE PURPOSE OF THIS SCHOOL IS TO CAUSE LEARNING

When Brian Roberts interviewed for the position of middle school principal, he and the other candidates for the job went through a long, detailed, demanding series of interviews. The school district Human Resources Department screened all applicants online and in person. The superintendent and other school district officials screened superior candidates in person based on input from Human Resources and the online applications.

A committee at the school conducted two rounds of interviews. This committee included the assistant principal, who would retire in one year and had not applied for this job, a school counselor, one teacher from each grade level, the librarian, an elective teacher, two parents/guardians, plus one staff member.

At the conclusion of his second interview with the school committee, Roberts was asked if he had any other thoughts he would like to express. He did. "Yes, thanks for the opportunity to express one more thought. It's all about learning. School is all about learning, or it's not a school, or it is a semi-school that is going in various directions. Schools exist because students need to learn. When schools 100 percent concentrate on the work that results in each student learning, we all win."

"If I become the principal of this school, we will be all about learning. Everyone will learn. Our entire school and our school community will learn. It will be our reason for being, and nothing will be allowed to reduce or dilute our relentless concentration on learning. If you want a school that has a total commitment to learning, then select me, and let's make that happen together." Brian Roberts got the job.

His first day on the job was a time for Mr. Roberts to begin learning and to begin causing learning. He began this job on July 15, so very few people were at school, but the custodians were there, as was the bookkeeper, and a few teachers. Brian talked to everyone; he walked through a few streets of the neighborhood and met some students plus some parents. Back at school, he sent an e-mail to all teachers and staff:

"I am honored to be the principal of this fine school. I look forward to working with you. I need your help with a project that will be completed soon. Let's create a theme—no, a goal—no, let's call it a 'purpose.' What is the purpose of our middle school? Please send me your thoughts. We will discuss all ideas when we meet a week before schools starts. Thank you."

Ideas came in during the next two weeks as people checked their e-mail from home, came to school and checked e-mail, or just heard what colleagues were talking about. When Brian met with the faculty and staff in August, he had compiled all of the ideas, and he had already e-mailed the full list to everyone. The ideas were discussed in the meeting of faculty and staff. One teacher of thirty-one years listened to the discussion and then spoke. Everyone listened whenever this dean of the faculty spoke.

"Mr. Roberts, I've been here a long time. This is one of the few times that a principal asked everyone for their ideas and then actually listened to us. It means a lot. You are off to a good start in my book. Oh, yes, if you look at all of the ideas we sent to you and if you listen closely to what has been said today, the words that keep coming up are 'students,' 'teaching,' and 'learning.' Our purpose is to teach all students so they all learn all of the curriculum."

The instant applause was sincere and was certain. The wording would be polished a bit, but the idea that the school's purpose would communicate had been identified. Every decision and every action at this school from then on would be devoted to and guided by the idea that the school's purpose was to teach all students so they all learn all of the curriculum.

Teachers, school counselors, school administrators, staff members, parents, guardians, students, community members, and school district officials saw fantastic results come from this school. Why? How? The answer is that this school was powered by a shared purpose that was created at the grassroots level and that was implemented of and by the grassroots level to get results of, by, and for everyone at the grassroots level.

Mr. Roberts's school created a community where people worked together to fulfill the school purpose. There is no top-down reform needed at this successful school community because the grassroots work has improved this school to a level beyond a level that top-down reforms perceive as possible. It should be unthinkable to impose a top-down reform on a school that is already accomplishing more than top-down reforms attempt to or can accomplish. To the extent that schools improve themselves through grassroots efforts that cause learning, the calls for top-down reform could begin to fade away.

Current educators can do more to improve schools than any other group. This is true for several reasons, including: (1) current educators, especially teachers, are where education happens, and (2) current educators know from their daily work experience what schools are doing well and what schools need to do better. The impact that current educators have at school each day is unsurpassed among all factors that educators can control or can influence to improve schools.

Be heard. Politicians, superintendents, school board members, community leaders need to hear from current educators, especially those teachers, counselors, and administrators who work at school every day. People who propose and advocate top-down, political, bureaucratic, systemic reforms of education need to hear from you about why those reforms do not work. They also need to hear from you about what does work, about what reality at school is, about what needs to be improved, and about how that can be improved.

Be involved. Current educators can participate in the school and in the community in ways that expand their impact.

Teachers: teach magnificently so learning is caused. That is the ultimate way to improve schools.

Principals: lead to relentlessly support the efforts of everyone at your school, yourself included, that cause learning.

12

The Power of Shared School Purpose

What happens if school is all about school, meaning if school is all about learning? Not about social engineering, not about excuses, not about using schools to address societal inequities, which schools are not designed to address, not about politics, not about power, and not about ego? Is that too idealistic to seek? No, the concept of education is built upon a foundation of many essential parts; one of which is idealism.

Create a mental picture of what you envision the typical school to look like, sound like, and have going on there during a typical school day. Your mental picture includes students, teachers, and classrooms. You may envision hallways, a library, the cafeteria, computers, lockers, an office, many people moving in many directions to get to many places. You may envision some classrooms where superior work is being done and other classrooms where little work is being done.

You may think of athletic teams, clubs, and activities. You may have a picture that includes most students behaving well and other students getting in trouble. You may see books, posters, DVD players, laptop computers, and, probably against the rules, cell phones. You have a picture of a place where different people are there for different reasons in pursuit of different goals.

If some people at this school are asked what they intend to accomplish each day at school, what their goal at school is, or what their opinion of school is, what would they say?

> Student 1: I come to see my friends. I go to class, but I really care more about seeing my friends.
>
> Student 2: I'm here to do whatever it takes to earn a college scholarship. My family cannot pay for me to go to college. I really want to be a lawyer, so I have

to go to college and then law school. I'm making good grades. I never get in trouble, and I'm involved in a lot of school stuff. I need to get all the scholarships I can get.

Student 3: All I intend to accomplish is to stay out of trouble and pass my classes. I never like school. My parents said, if I graduated from high school, they would buy me a car. All I need is to pass classes and not get suspended. That's all I do here.

Student 4: I intend to be a basketball star. A real star. All I care about at school is sports. I play basketball, and just to get in better shape, I run on the track team. I make average grades, so the coaches never have to worry about me or bother me. My goal is to play college basketball for one or two years and then play professional basketball. Nothing else gets my attention except my friends sometimes.

Student 5: School is not bad. Actually, it is pretty good most days. My teachers are good. I'm in some neat clubs. I'm in the marching band. I make good grades. I come here to do my work and have some fun.

Teacher 1: I arrive early. I stay late. I take school very seriously. I take each student very seriously. I write college letters of recommendation for students, and I spend a lot of time on each of those letters. I serve on a school committee, the curriculum committee. I never put up with students who refuse to work. I find something good that motivates them, and we use that. I stay in touch with parents and guardians to tell them good news or bad news about what their child is doing. I'm here every day to be a great teacher.

Teacher 2: I take this work seriously. I also take my family seriously. I put in about fifty hours at school each week. When I can, I do some more school work at home. I want all of my students to succeed. The problem is some of them work and some of them are lazy. They are in high school. They know what they are supposed to do. They got in habits years ago. Some have always worked hard, behaved, and learned.

Others just get by. Others do nothing for class and cause a lot of trouble. I wish everyone worked and behaved, but the problems some of these students bring with them are too much for any one teacher to solve when we have classes of twenty-five or thirty students.

Teacher 3: I am going to retire in one year. The truth is, I just want to finish this one year and move on. I'm not so old, but I sure am tired. We keep getting asked to do more every year. Solve all of society's problems is what it seems we are told. Then every few years, we are told to change everything we are doing. Well, in one year, another big change is coming, but I will be gone before that starts.

Teacher 4: This is my first year of teaching. It is harder than I expected, but I really like it. I worked hard in college to help pay for college and then for my graduate degree right after college. Being a teacher is the only work I'm interested in. I'm doing all I can to be a really good teacher.

Teacher 5: I've been a teacher for fifteen years. I'm a good teacher. Others are better; others are worse. I'm thirty-eight years old, so it would be tough to change careers. I hope I can get more excited about the next fifteen years than I have been about the past few years. I don't want to become one of those old, cranky teachers who complain all the time, but I have to admit, there is a lot to complain about.

School counselor: I come here every day hoping I can help students deal with problems and make good decisions and find some wonderful opportunities. Most days there is something to cry about and something else to be happy about. This is what I do. I think the students need me, so I am thankful to work here.

Secretary: This is the busiest place in town. People come and go all day. The phone rings constantly. I try to be friendly and helpful to everyone. I might be the first impression someone has of our school, so I want that to be a good impression.

Custodian: It's hard work at a school. Things get broken. The place gets dirty. Problems come up. I do my best to help everyone. I wish we had more supplies and equipment. I have a friend who is the head custodian at a big mall. They have all the equipment you can imagine. I think we ought to be able to take care of a school better than we take care of a mall.

Cafeteria manager: We feed about 2,050 students each day at lunch and 450 at breakfast. My staff works hard. They really care about the students. I wish the students would say "thank you" more often, not to me but to my staff. They work hard, and they deserve some appreciation.

Principal: My job says I'm supposed to be the instructional leader. That rarely happens. I'm the crisis manager, the chief emergency officer, the personnel manager, the law enforcement director, the policy enforcer, the livid-parent negotiator, the out-of-control-student miracle worker, and a lot more. Who else can deal with all of this stuff that comes up? I do all of that. On a good day, I keep the place from falling apart. On a bad day, I put the place back together.

Those fifteen people have quite a variety of answers to the topic of what they intend to accomplish at school each day, or what their goal at school is, or what their opinion of school is. If the other 2,200 people at school were asked their thoughts, the range of answers would probably broaden.

How can an organization function at peak performance if the 2,215 people who are there move in different directions toward various and sometimes conflicting or contradictory goals? How can this school be improved if the grassroots reality is that there are 2,215 different perceptions of the purpose of a school or, at least, of the purpose that school serves for each individual?

The productivity of a grassroots effort to improve a school is enhanced if everyone involved in the school is in agreement with the purpose of the school and if everyone involved with the school improvement work directs their endeavors to fulfilling the school purpose.

What would people at a school that is dedicated to a unifying and shared school purpose—to cause learning—and is dedicated to continuous school improvement at the grassroots level say that they intend to accomplish each day at school, say is their goal for their work at school, and say is their opinion of school? By this point in this book, the reader is equipped with the answer to the above questions, so space is provided for the reader to write the answer:

Student 1:

Student 2:

Student 3:

Student 4:

Student 5:

Teacher 1:

Teacher 2:

Teacher 3:

Teacher 4:

Teacher 5:

School counselor:

Secretary:

Custodian:

Cafeteria manager:

Principal:

Now see how your thoughts above match up with the following version:

Student 1: We got a new principal last year. All he ever talks about is learning. When we wait for a bus after school, he asks us what we learned that day. When he sees us at a football game, he asked us what we learned that day. He really is serious about all of this learning.

Student 2: I'm not real crazy about school. I never have been. I just want to finish and get out of here. There's just not much to do here that I care about except for that new class this year about money management. The teachers last year asked us what we would like to learn, and enough people mentioned money that the new class was started.

Student 3: What do I try to accomplish at school? Well, the commercials on the morning school news say I'm supposed to learn all the time. That is not what I do all the time because I like visiting with my friends. I learn a lot. I want to be ready for college. I need to earn a scholarship. Learning is fine with me.

Student 4: I am going to keep making great grades. I need to get a full ride to college. I'm a good soccer player but not college-scholarship good. I'm smart but not a genius, so I have to work harder than other students. I want to be a doctor and find a cure for cancer because my uncle was really sick with cancer and he almost died. I need help paying for that, so I need great grades. I am reading a lot on my own for an independent study class.

Our high school does not teach about cancer, but a biology teacher is my mentor for my independent study on cancer. It's pretty neat to learn about what I'm interested in. It's like the signs at our school tell us—learn, learn more, keep learning, or something like that.

Student 5: School has become so serious. We are told every day in each class to learn. I get the point. I know that's what teachers have to do, and I'm willing to learn. I'd like a few more classes that relate to my interests. I'm all about computers, but we have one computer class. I might get to take a college computer class when I'm a senior next year. That would be cool. I want to learn all about computers and someday design new smart phones and music players. If I can learn that at this school, I'll get more serious about learning.

Teacher 1: The school communicates what we are supposed to do every day. The goal of this school is learning, all day, every day. Our job is to be sure that everyone learns. Our principal tells us all the time. Our school letterhead tells people. Our signs around school tell people. This is the school where everyone learns.

Teacher 2: Teaching is hard work, harder than ever. I've been at it twenty-two years. I've seen trends come and go. I've seen laws come and go. I've seen principals come and go. I've seen superintendents go a lot. They don't stay very long.

Anyway, I just try to keep up. We get told to do more stuff every year. We get told about new tests every year. We get told to give more students second and third chances, but those students just won't work. What can I do to force them to learn if they refuse to do any work at all?

Teacher 3: I will retire in two years. What's my goal? Truth: my goal is to get through those two years, but deep down inside I really want to do more. It's my last two years, but it's the only time these students will be in high school. So I told the principal I needed something to get me motivated. He asked if there were some other classes I would like to teach besides ninth-grade civics. Well, of course.

I would like to teach United States history to juniors and United States government to seniors. As it worked out, a teacher who had those classes was interested in teaching ninth grade, so we switched. I can't wait for next year. The students are going to learn so much. Maybe I'll delay retirement? No way, but I'll do my best teaching ever between now and when I retire.

Teacher 4: I have taught for thirty-one years. I'm only fifty-three years old. Who retires at fifty-three? I'd like to try school administration before I retire, but I'll quit immediately if the laws change one more time. I can get my students to learn. I have always been able to do that.

But if the governor gets his way or maybe it's the commissioner of education or maybe it is someone else who is really powerful, but if they pass that law telling me I have to follow an exact day-to-day scripted class routine, I'll quit. That stuff is not teaching. It's, I don't know, it turns us all into robots instead of teachers and students.

Teacher 5: I do my job very well. I will gladly keep doing this job well. Just keep those so-called experts who can't teach from coming here and telling me how to teach.

School counselor: This school is all about learning. I teach students how to schedule their classes, how to cope with problems, how to get along with people, how to stay out of trouble, how to get a job, how to get into college. I teach everything a counselor can teach. I make it a point to get out of my office many times a day so I can be in hallways, in the cafeteria, in a classroom, in the library. I minimize office time because the office is not where school happens and it is not where 99 percent of the learning happens.

We challenge the most gifted students. We encourage the students who make C grades to work up to B grades. We provide support and interventions for students who are at risk of failing a class. We have a great drop-out prevention program, which combines helping students and pestering the same students when they get lazy or silly.

We deal seriously with the 5 percent of students who cause 95 percent of the discipline problems. They are shocked when we tell them they don't have the right to interfere with the work teachers do and the learning other students do. If they will not cooperate, we get them placed in the alternative school so they can succeed there and so our school can be a school.

Secretary: Well, this school is all about learning. When I answer the phone I say, "Hello. This is Wilson High School where everyone learns." When people walk in the office, they see the banner that says, "We cause learning." That usually gets a reaction. I manage the office. My goal is to keep the office running smoothly, but the school is all about learning.

It's starting to catch on. We say it so much. You know, there is something like a commercial that sticks in your mind going on here. We really are creating a school atmosphere where what we say is what we do. It really is all about learning here. It's just what we do. I think that's true at most schools, but we make sure it is true here.

Custodian: It's been different here the past year or so. I used to watch students in the cafeteria not clean up after themselves or not take their trays back. That doesn't happen much now. This place has a feeling about it now. The principal challenged the students.

He said that many of them were concerned about pollution and recycling and other earth stuff, but they did not take care of their own school the way they thought people should take care of this planet. I guess they learned something about themselves. We still have a lot of custodial work to do, but the students and teachers really do help keep this place looking good.

Cafeteria manager: It meant a lot to me last year when a health teacher invited me to speak to a class about nutrition. The cafeteria staff and I know a lot about food, but in my twenty-three years of working here, that was the first time a teacher asked me to talk to a class. Now I go to health classes regularly to tell them about nutrition. They seem eager to learn. Plus, I get their ideas for the cafeteria. I learned from the students, and we made some changes they suggested. It's just how things work here now. We all work together and learn together.

Principal: I come to school every day with two major goals. First, everyone learns. Tied for first, the place is safe. Some students think that if you steal a $300 cell phone from somebody at school, it is not a crime because it happened at school. They think it just breaks a school rule. Wrong. We take issues like that to the court system. It's a chore sometimes to put in the time to prosecute for theft or disorderly conduct, which is what a fight at school is, but we get results.

Theft is rare here, and fights are very rare. We have taught these students that crime is not determined by location. If you steal at a store, it's a crime. If you steal at school, it's a crime. It helps keep this school safe. It also reinforces that we are here to learn. If you insist on being a criminal, we insist that you do not attend this school. There is an alternative school, and we get the repeat offenders placed there to get their education. The taxpayers pay a fortune to operate this school, and it is going to be a school, not a place to steal or fight.

The students in psychology classes use me as an example when they talk about obsessions. They say I have an obsession with learning. They are right. I tell them it is a total commitment and a complete dedication. But it is true that the sermon we preach at this school every day is that we are here to learn; all of us, students and adults, are here every day to learn together, to create learning, to cause learning. Nothing is allowed to get in the way of that.

I expect myself to lead by example, so I get into every classroom at least once a week and so do the assistant principals. We help teach whenever a teacher asks us to. I eat lunch with students and find out what they are learning. And I say "no" to any use of time or resources that fails to fully support the learning goal of this school. This place is all about learning all the time.

It has helped that sponsors of clubs and coaches of sports stress what needs to be learned. If you know everything there is to know about a sport, it makes you a better participant in the sport. Our soccer coaches make each soccer player get certified as a soccer referee. Why? Because referees watch the game differently from how players or coaches do. And if you know the rules of the game like a referee does, you obey the rules, and you just understand the whole concept of the sport better.

The sponsor of our Recycling and Environment Club begins each meeting with a student presenting the results of research about a way other schools, cities, companies, and nations are dealing with environmental issues. They learn at each meeting, and they have fun being together to do stuff, but they do learn.

So, we are not perfect, but we are getting great results. The faculty and staff, the parents and guardians seem very pleased. The students know they are part of a very good school, and that means something. One student told me that she recently got hired at a local store, and the reason was that she goes to school here.

The store owner has heard about our wonderful obsession with learning, with hard work, with good behavior. The store owner told her that if she went to school here, she should be a good employee if she does everything at work the way we do things at school. When students realize that what we are doing here can help them get a job now, well, that can make a real impression.

Now, I should add that the teachers and I realize that the school district has responsibilities, so they have to check on what we are doing. Sometimes they have to tell us about new mandates or policies. We comply with all of that.

The teachers and I realize that a lot of funds for schools come through the state government, so there are state laws and state regulations to follow. We do all of that. School district officials and state government officials are welcome at this school anytime. We just ask for the opportunity to reason together.

This school is unique. Each school is unique. Solutions and successes can happen at each school, but how that happens will vary from school to school. We just ask that the results we are getting here, which surpass all statistical goals the state set and the school district set, be the major factor in discussions about what we need to change, if anything.

Top-down, political, bureaucratic, systemic reform of education does not work. Such reform initiatives last for a few years, fail, and these are followed by further, similar reform initiatives.

Grassroots efforts to improve schools can work and do work. They address the heart of, the essence of and the purpose of schools—to cause learning—where that is done: in classrooms at schools, in all other parts of or activities at school, and in every proper way that proper school work can be supported. We know what works. We know what does not work. Let's do only what works.

When schools cause learning, there is no need for top-down reforms to be considered because schools are already doing what is expected. When the people at the grassroots level and people who can support those at the grassroots level—the school, the families associated with the school, the people who work at the school, the students at the school, the community in which the school is located, business leaders and owners, media, community groups, politicians, citizens, governments, former educators, and current educators—listen to each other and work together toward implementing the purpose of a school, to cause learning, the results can be outstanding.

Those outstanding results and school improvements, of, by, and for the grassroots, benefit everyone and are obtained without the costs and the counterproductive, political, bureaucratic, systemic misdirection of top-down reforms.

Education happens in classrooms at schools. Top-down education reform doesn't work. Grassroots efforts to improve schools can provide answers and results. Schools are improved with effective actions where education happens, not where power pyramids peak.

13

The Great Debate: The Reformers Respond and the Grass Roots Reply

Top-down, political, bureaucratic, systemic reform of education has its advocates. There are political candidates and elected officials whose campaign promises include sincere statements about solving the problems of education through changes in state law and through changes in how state government manages, measures, monitors, and motivates schools.

There are community groups, business groups, and interest groups that support reforms of education that are consistent with the goals of their groups. A community group that is involved in civil rights or equity issues may support systemic reform of education due to a perception that schools provide more effective services to one group of students than to another group of students. A business group may have attempted to work with a school or with schools, and faced with their goals still not met, the business group worked with school district, state, and/or national government officials on education reform.

Some people who work in education may seek top-down political reform to reverse prior top-down political reform of education. Other educators may have worked up the chain of command to change schools, but were not able to get their desired results. They decided to change strategy and tactics by taking their energies further up the education and political hierarchy to impose change where there had been resistance.

Local school district officials—school board members or superintendents—can feel the pressure of national government supervision or state government monitoring. Seeing a range of results from the schools in the district, these officials may consider system-wide mandates as a way to fulfill their obligations and to get better results from schools.

Despite repeated attempts and implementations, there has not been a perfect top-down reform of education that was universally recognized as the ultimate, long-awaited ideal. The history of education reform is a history of reform following reform.

The advocates of top-down education reform might say that each successive reform seeks to build on prior successes. The opponents of top-down education reform might say that each prior reform failed and that each successive reform will show that reform continues to fall short of its promises. A direct debate between these two perspectives could be revealing, so let the direct debate begin.

> Moderator: We welcome everyone in this very large crowd to our first community convention. The public was invited, and it is wonderful that the public is here. Our topic tonight is education. Our community leaders have, through the school board and through work with state government, set some very ambitious goals for our schools. The debate tonight will address the best ways to reach those goals.
>
> One side will contend that a large systemic change is needed and that this must be imposed by local and/or state reform action. The other side will contend that education is improved from the bottom up and that real improvement comes primarily from actions taken at the classroom level and/or at the school level. The debate participants will introduce themselves in their opening statements. The audience is asked to listen politely, not to cheer or to interrupt our speakers. If time permits, we may be able to take a few questions from the audience after this debate. Based on a coin toss, the advocate of systemic reform will give the first opening statement.
>
> Reformer: Welcome to everyone in attendance tonight and to everyone watching the complete televised coverage of this debate on the local public access cable television channel. I am Caroline Austin. I was an elementary school teacher for eleven years and then an elementary school principal for thirteen years before becoming an assistant superintendent for seven years.
>
> Since I retired from public education six years ago, I have been the vice-president of a consulting leadership development firm. In this capacity, I often serve as a consultant to school districts and to state governments with major emphasis on systemic reform of education. I also work with a political consulting group to advise candidates for state offices and for the United States Congress as they develop their education policies.
>
> Grass roots: I would like to welcome everyone to this important gathering. My name is Justin Lawrence. I have been a middle school teacher, assistant principal, and principal for twenty-three years. During the past four years, I have served as my school district's director of curriculum, testing, and professional development, but I do not work in the district's central office.
>
> I am in one of our school district's fourteen schools each day. I rotate through the fourteen schools and then begin that fourteen-day rotation again. My reason for this is to be where the students, teachers, principals, counselors, and staff

are. The vital work of education is not done in offices or in hierarchies. The vital work of education is done at schools.

Moderator: Our first topic gets to the heart of the matter. Top down or bottom up? Everyone would like to see schools improve, but there is strong disagreement about how to do this. What makes the top-down education reform approach or the bottom-up school improvement approach better?

Reformer: That is an excellent question, and in many ways, it is the essential question. What you call "top-down education reform" is what my consulting colleagues and I call "structured and directed educational management." Our experience is that as education has become a more complex and complicated process, which involves everything from national law to state regulation to local policies, the top-down approach is the only structured and directed way to implement educational changes in a consistent and fair manner.

Top-down may imply, but it does not always mean, that the national government impersonally mandates exactly what each state must do in its school system. For that matter, top-down does not always mean that the state government impersonally imposes exactly what each school district must do.

Top-down, what we call "structured and directed educational management," could be seen in the actions taken by a local school board, which every school must follow. A school district superintendent or a school principal may need to do his or her job using some directives that everyone in lower levels must abide by. The goals of efficiency, continuity, consistency, and fairness are honorable goals that structured and directed school management enhances.

Any person in a position of leadership duties is obligated to get results. That leader, any leader, must be able to impact what is done and sometimes to control what is done. If you are responsible for the results, you have to be given some or much of the authority to get the results.

Whether it is the bottom-line profit of a business or the bottom-line test scores of students, there are executives in the educational system and in the political system who must lead and who must manage. Those executives are in high-ranking positions of authority and responsibility. They have access to vital information. They can find the best actions to take, and then they can implement those actions consistently throughout the area where they have jurisdiction. Other approaches have far too little accountability, oversight, and coordinated operation of approved actions.

Grass roots: We just heard the very convincing reasons why the top-down approach is not the better option. The reformers use rigid structure, dominating direction, micromanagement, and, far too often, misleadership instead of leadership. The executives mentioned moments ago never teach one student, yet they eloquently speak about the urgency of making sure that each student learns.

What evidence indicates that a new executive order or directive is the ideal way to make sure that every student in every classroom impacted by the order or the directive learns the most that he or she can learn?

What evidence supports the bottom-up or grassroots approach to improve education? Ask students what has been most important to them in their educational experience. They will tell you about a teacher who deeply cared, who relentlessly worked, never gave up on the student, who never let the student give up on himself or herself, who challenged the student, and who creatively found a teaching method that intrigued and inspired the student. Students will not tell you about directives, structures, or management.

Ask teachers what is done that most supports and enhances their work with students in terms of what a school system can provide. Will those teachers speak of how helpful certain directives or structures were? Or will those teachers speak of school administrators who spent meaningful time in classrooms, who provided encouragement, guidance, constructive criticism, support, and answers?

Will those teachers speak of a support system in the school and in the school district that makes sure that the computers work, the copy machines work, the heat and air conditioning system works, the textbooks are sufficient for each student to have one, and that teacher-written discipline referrals about students' misbehavior are taken seriously and are acted upon promptly?

Will those teachers mention that they were allowed to attend, maybe to create, useful professional development programs instead of generic, pointless programs that some high-ranking officials decided everyone must endure?

If you must think of education as a hierarchy with governors and commissioners of education at the top, then you will put schools and classrooms at the bottom. How many students does a governor teach? None. How many teachers or principals does a state's commissioner of education work with directly on a typical day? Very few, if any.

The real work of education is for students to learn. That is done in schools and in classrooms. That means schools and classrooms are the places where educational improvement must happen because those are the only places where real educational improvement can happen. The people who work in schools and in classrooms do more for education every day than any top-down process ever can because those people are where education happens.

Moderator: Do you see some benefit of and some possibility of compromise? Could there be a combination of far-reaching, broad political and systemic reform of education combined with grassroots efforts that emphasize what is done in classrooms and in schools? Is there some moderate hybrid that gets the best of both approaches?

Grass roots: That would be a very delicate balancing act because the top-down approach is, for the most part, contradictory to the grassroots approach. Any reform that is imposed from the top-down, by definition, directs what is to be done at schools and in classrooms despite the reality that one size of a solution does not fit the variety of sizes of problems within each school and each classroom.

In the high school teacher's daily work, she may use different teaching methods and activities with each class she teaches. She knows her students, and she makes adjustments as needed. If a top-down approach mandated that certain actions had to be done in precisely prescribed ways in every classroom, the individuality of each student and the uniqueness of each class would be sacrificed to the limitations of uniformity, which are so often included in top-down reforms.

I fully understand the obligations and the duties of superintendents and governors to see that tax dollars are spent wisely. I also realize that the public schools are subject to the political processes of compromises, constitutions, laws, regulations, and policies. I welcome monitoring of the work done in classrooms and in schools. Oversight of schools is part of the duty of government and is part of the obligation government has to taxpayers.

Let's try this comparison. There are government health care programs to help people pay for and get health care. Those programs are monitored, and there is much oversight. When a medical doctor is conducting a surgery on the patient, is the physician making adjustments based on the reality of what this one particular patient needs, or must the surgery be done exactly the same way for every patient?

When a teacher is working with a student or with a class, is the teacher given the freedom to make adjustments, or must the teacher follow a precisely scripted or rigidly controlled set of procedures with little or no variation allowed?

So, the suggestion that top-down reform and grassroots school improvement could be blended into a smooth compromise is just not very practical.

Reformer: I may be more optimistic about the hybrid idea or about a best-of-both-worlds compromise, but I would suggest that the greater portion of any compromise needs to be the top-down reform part. We are not in our current educational crisis because of too much control from the state government or from the school district. There is much room for additional control and uniformity and directed management.

We already know that no two teachers are doing exactly the same thing and that no two schools are doing exactly the same thing. I would propose that such lack of uniformity is a big part of the reason that we have underperforming schools.

Let's find out what the best teachers in the country are doing, and then let's require every teacher to do the same thing. Let's find out what the best principals in the country are doing, and then let's make all principals do that. If there is a best way to do something, then that way should be the only way we allow.

It takes a lot of organizational thoroughness to implement the ideals of uniformity. Teachers have to be observed regularly and often to confirm that the required teaching methods, activities, pace, schedule, and documentation conform to the requirements. Lesson plans, tests, homework, grades, communication with families, this cannot be left to chance.

Administrators at each school must closely monitor all of this, and the people those administrators report to must make sure that the reports from the administrators are correct and are confirmed. People may not like the word "bureaucracy," but that's what it takes to be sure that everyone at the classroom level and at the school level is doing the required work according to acceptable standards of measured performance. So, my experience, my training, and my judgment caution against expecting much harmony in the type of hybrid or compromise that was suggested.

Moderator: There are many ideas about how to get better schools. What are the best sources of the best ideas?

Reformer: You are so right. There are many sources of useful ideas about how to reform schools. My colleagues and I pay close attention to position papers that are published by think tanks. We know that some of these groups have a political agenda. We know that these think tanks often have a strong allegiance with the conservative political philosophy or with the liberal political philosophy while a few others are moderate.

Still, we find it very helpful to read these think tank position papers, which are often quite insightful and scholarly while also being certain in specific recommendations about public policy. The think tank experts spend all of their time on research and analysis. They are a resource that simply must be used.

We also find the fifty state governments to be important sources of ideas and innovations. Many significant education reform programs have been initiated at the state level by governors, state legislators, state education officials, state boards of education, and interest groups in states. To be aware of what each state is doing to reform education is to make yourself knowledgeable of fifty important and different approaches.

I have told some clients that they could take the best idea from each of the fifty states and create an exceptional education reform plan. What happens more commonly is for a state government to borrow more heavily from one or two states that have implemented a proven reform package, but even then, some additional ideas from other states or from think tanks can get included.

I do think it is very helpful to read the national education publications and the state publications about education. There are so many professional educator groups of teachers or administrators or professors that publish scholarly journals and monthly or quarterly magazines. These are filled with updates, reports, articles, analysis, and commentary.

We keep up with new books in the field of education. It is amazing how much gets published each year about schools. These sources help keep us aware of emerging ideas. The same is true for dissertations that come from doctoral programs in graduate schools of education. The research that goes into those dissertations is very revealing. So those are some sources of very good ideas, innovations, and reforms.

Grass roots: Did you notice what was missing from the answer we just heard? Think about that as you listen to my answer, please.

The question is what are the best sources of the best ideas about how to get better schools? The answer is in schools. Is there a better think tank than a classroom where outstanding teaching is creating unlimited learning? No, that is the best think tank of all.

If you want to know how to realistically improve schools, go to real schools that have improved. See what is being done there that is getting great results. Notice the benefit. You get to find out about something that actually works in the classroom setting in a real school. You then take that idea and action to your classroom in your school and implement it so it works for your students, which means you adjust it based on the realities and uniqueness of your students.

Every school has its best teachers or its groups of highest quality teachers. The people who are great teachers usually are eager to become even better, so give them opportunities to observe in each other's classrooms, and give them time to trade ideas with each other. For teachers who are average or who are below average, there are other teachers in the same school who are very good or great.

Create ways at the school level for the average or below average teachers to get great ideas and mentoring from the better teachers. This is person to person, colleague to colleague and is direct human interaction. No think tank reports or state government task force reports are needed when the great teacher in classroom 200 shares ideas with, answers questions from, and mentors the average teacher in classroom 201.

My experience is that the same approach works with principals and assistant principals. In each school district, there are superior school administrators who can provide ideas, guidance, and mentoring to new principals or to any school administrator who can do better work than he or she is doing now.

Why use a vague, generic analysis of leadership and management theories when a colleague in a nearby school can provide practical, proven, realistic guidance, answers, direction, and solutions?

The best ideas are those that are already getting the best results in classrooms and in schools. Go ask great teachers and great principals what they are doing that works best. You will get a real answer that can be applied, as adjusted, to meet your unique situation, very quickly and efficiently.

Moderator: We see new laws about education from the national government and from state governments. Are there times when these governments just have to take charge and insist on change, mandate change, and impose changes through the force of law, regulations, rewards, and penalties?

Grass roots: My questions would be: what is the motive, what is the goal, and what else, if anything else, has been tried? If the motive is someone's political career and the advantage he or she seeks in the political arena, then I would be very, very suspicious.

If a candidate or an officeholder uses education reform for personal political gain, then it is offensive to reasonable people. That candidate may merely be listening to political strategists or campaign managers who insist that a major statewide education reform will play well with the voters and will enable the candidate to own the education issue.

If a governor and the state legislature are at odds over education laws and they let their political power battles play out through deliberations and negotiations on education reform, the strongest motive could be to win the political battle rather than to improve schools. What assurance do we have that great ideas will emerge from the collision of political egos, disagreements, and ambitions?

What is the goal of the imposed changes you mentioned? Is it to strengthen the power of the state education bureaucracy? Is it to maneuver one potential candidate into a better political position than another potential candidate? Is the goal to improve the educational experience of every student in kindergarten through high school? If that is the goal, then the emphasis must be on the kindergarten through high school classrooms and schools.

Consider this, please. Did you ever have a teacher who gave every student a copy of the classroom rules and it amounted to page after page of rules, yet, the teacher had almost no control over the class? She would add new rules, but nothing got better.

Then think of another teacher you had whose list of rules was quite clear but much shorter. This teacher had superior control of the classroom. Her rules were enforced, but there was little misbehavior. Why? Because she so fascinated her students with challenging and energetic and useful learning experiences that the students concentrated on their work, not on what mischief they could get away with.

My point is, you could add more laws and regulations forever, but don't we have enough already? Do we have a shortage of laws and regulations about schools? No, we have an abundance of them. If the national government or the state governments or school boards impose more laws, regulations, and policies, why do they expect great results when prior laws, regulations, and policies, which were supposed to fix schools, apparently did not fix the schools? And those political reforms are always so short term. The reform gets passed, and everything changes. Then a new reform gets passed, and everything changes again.

Stop that waste of time and effort and money, which the reform merry-go-round always absorbs. Let schools concentrate on teaching and learning, not on filling out forms to comply with some new, short-term reform.

So the answer is "no." There is not a convincing reason to complicate matters by adding more bureaucratic stuff for schools to comply with. Liberate schools from all of that. Let schools be schools, not political pawns or social engineering laboratories.

Reformer: The answer is "yes." There are times when changes in education practices have to be imposed on all schools in a certain jurisdiction. It might be throughout a state or throughout a school district. Someday, it might be even more than the national government has done thus far to impact what has been done in schools.

The answer is "yes" because of fairness. It should not matter which school a student attends in a school district or in a state. Maybe we can extend that to say it should not matter which school anywhere in the nation a student attends. The point is that every school must be good, and that means some actions must be imposed or mandated.

It makes no sense in terms of fairness for a student to get a great education in one school, but another student gets an ordinary or worse education in a school that is only miles away from the great school. That's where consistent, uniform, structured educational procedures and standards must be imposed.

The answer is also "yes" for the realistic reason that not everyone seeks to do great work and not everyone is willing to go the extra mile through his or her own personal initiative. An acceptable standard of work must be imposed on some people, educators included.

It would be lovely to think otherwise, but let's be realistic. For the people who just do enough work to not get fired, higher standards have to be imposed by law or regulation, and then that has to be rigidly enforced through thorough monitoring and frequent evaluation.

Moderator: One more question, and that will conclude our prepared questions. Then we will have time for two or three questions from the audience. Perhaps leadership is a major factor in the process of improving schools. Governors certainly are in a position to lead. Principals are in a position to lead. If we agree that schools need to get better, where is the best source of leadership or the best position of leadership on this?

Reformer: Leadership is strengthened when it is combined with authority. The governor of a state has the authority to execute the laws of that state, including the laws about education. That is a unique position of political, legal, and executive authority.

State legislators can lead, and with their authority to shape bills, to approve bills, or to oppose bills, they have important authority on many issues including education. The same would be true for school board members in terms of shaping, approving, or opposing policies at the local school district level.

School district superintendents have many opportunities to lead. They have much organizational authority because they are the highest-ranking employee in the school district. They can strengthen their leadership impact by the example they set. How they use their time will reveal what their priorities are.

Principals are known to sometimes feel more like managers than leaders. There is so much at a school that has to be managed, and some of that can be done only by the principal. Even if the principal delegates duties, he or she still has the bottom line responsibility for everything that happens at a school. Still, if a principal has the job under control and does not let events control him or her, there is much room in the principal's job description for leadership.

Grass roots: Teachers, school counselors, principals, and assistant principals are the most important leaders in education. Teachers do not always perceive themselves as leaders, but they are the instructional leaders in their classrooms. All characteristics of leaders can be applied by teachers in their work. Here's one example. Leaders use this standard: results, not excuses.

There is a long list of explanations about why some students fail in school or do very poor work in class, but the best of teachers think and work in terms of getting results, not accepting excuses. This does not mean that we expect teachers to do the impossible. Some patients need to see a physician who is a specialist. Some students may need to go to a specialty or alternative school.

Still, most students who most teachers work with will respond positively to a variety of creative teaching methods and activities that are fueled with enthusiasm, challenges, and connections with real life.

Principals, assistant principals, and school counselors can and should be leaders in their schools. This does not mean that everyone in a school can have the authority or the duties of the principal. This does mean that leadership skills can be developed by everyone who works at a school.

For example, leaders listen. Principals, assistant principals, and school counselors at a school can attentively listen to people at the school. This is part of creating a school-wide atmosphere of listening to each other as a way to share good ideas, to mutually solve problems, and to create a sense of community.

Leaders take the initiative. Of course, this has to be done within the limits of a job description. A teacher cannot take the initiative to usurp the duties of a principal. A teacher can take the initiative to create new varied teaching methods and activities that break through barriers to learning faced by some students or which inspire some students to do the best work they have ever done.

Leadership is not owned exclusively by people who win elections or by people in certain jobs. Leadership methods can be used by anyone who will take the initiative to lead. A teacher can lead students to learning. There is nothing easy about that work, but it can be done, especially in a school where everyone who works there sees themselves as the people who can do the most to improve their school.

Moderator: We have heard some fascinating ideas. I would like to thank our participants in this debate for your enlightening thoughts and your very civil approach to this debate. Now, we do have time for two or three questions from the audience, so if you have a question, please step to the microphone.

Question 1: I graduated from high school about ten years ago. I remember that in middle school there were a lot of changes in school. Then I heard that a few years ago those changes were eliminated. My question is, was what I went through in school good, or was it so bad it had to be replaced?

Reformer: I do not know the specifics of those changes, but I would think that what you experienced was good but that better ideas emerged later. Education never stands still. Changes in schools are being made continuously.

Grass roots: I know what changes you are mentioning. There were many new ideas about middle school that were being implemented, and some of those worked their way up to be used in high school for ninth graders especially and for some tenth graders. The reason those new ideas went away was because of a triple play—a new governor, three new school board members in this school district, and a new superintendent in this school district.

The Great Debate: The Reformers Respond and the Grass Roots Reply   167

It might interest you to know that all of those people have moved on to other jobs or have ended their school board term. More changes are already being proposed by their successors. Unfortunately, that process continues, and far too often is change for the sake of change instead of change because of a better plan.

Question 2: I tend to support the idea that reform is needed because some people just don't do their jobs unless they are forced to. What do you think of that way of looking at things?

Grass roots: That is not my experience. The promise I made to myself years ago was to put heart and soul into this work. The educators and staff members I have worked with are also motivated to succeed, to get results, to make a difference for good in the lives of students. The staff members I have worked with saw the important contributions they could make and did their jobs with real dedication.

You may think of me as optimistic, but I have years of experience in education. That experience gives me the confidence to trust the people I work with. I do not trust naively. I trust because I have seen and continue to see conscientious and dedicated people do highly effective work.

Reformer: Your question and perception show very realistic insight. The truth is that not everyone who works in a school or in the education system does exemplary work or even average work. Of course, many people in education rise above all of the required standards. But other people do not, and because of them, we must have education reform which, among other things, gives education officials the options needed to be sure that people comply with job requirements.

Question 3: I've listened to everything said in this debate. I would suggest that there has to be a better way. It's not all reform or no reform. It's not all top down or all grassroots. I think we should reform whenever necessary and empower people at the grass roots to be more assertive. Why does it have to be one or the other if both could help?

Reformer: Very interesting question. My answer is that reform is fair, consistent, equitable, and uniform. Reform is the better option because it does what grassroots efforts cannot do.

Grass roots: Reform never works as promised despite good intentions of the reformers. Reform is superficial and temporary. Learning needs to be deep and permanent. Learning happens in classrooms, not in reform strategy sessions or in reform mandates.

Moderator: Thanks to our participants, our audience, and to people who have been watching on television. We all have very much to think about.

What questions would the reader ask of the debate participants, and what answers would be expected? Think about those topics, please.

Reader question 1:

Reformer answer:

Grass roots answer:

Reader question 2:

Reformer answer:

Grass roots answer:

What does the reader conclude? The premise of this book is that top-down, political, bureaucratic, systemic reform of education does not work but that grassroots efforts to improve schools can provide answers and can get results. What does the reader think?

About the Author

Keen J. Babbage has twenty-seven years of experience as a teacher and administrator in middle school, high school, college, and graduate school. He is the author of *911: The School Administrator's Guide to Crisis Management* (1996), *Meetings for School-Based Decision Making* (1997), *High-Impact Teaching: Overcoming Student Apathy* (1998), *Extreme Teaching* (2002), *Extreme Learning* (2004), *Extreme Students* (2005), *Results-Driven Teaching: Teach So Well That Every Student Learns* (2006), *Extreme Economics* (2007, 2009), *What Only Teachers Know about Education* (2008), *Extreme Writing* (2010), *The Extreme Principle* (2010), and *The Dream and Reality of Teaching* (2011).

CPSIA information can be obtained at www.ICGtesting.com
Printed in the USA
BVOW040546260412

288713BV00002B/3/P